WITHDRA

D1626670

31

Gilbert Harding

A CANDID PORTRAYAL

Wallace Reyburn

ANGUS & ROBERTSON
PUBLISHERS

ANGUS & ROBERTSON · PUBLISHERS

London · Sydney · Melbourne · Si

**COUNTY LIBRARY
TOWN CENTRE, TALLAGHT**

ACC. NO.   0207 957835
COPY NO.   TC 1005
INV. NO.   BACKSTCK
PRICE IR£   6·50
CLASS   920HARDING

This book is copyright. Apart from any fair
dealing for the purposes of private study,
research, criticism or review, as permitted
under the Copyright Act, no part may be
reproduced by any process without written
permission. Inquiries should be addressed
to the publisher.

First published by Angus and Robertson (UK) Ltd,
16 Ship Street, Brighton, Sussex in 1978

Copyright © Wallace Reyburn 1978

ISBN 0 207 95783 5

CO. DUBLIN
LIBRARY SERVICE
Acc. No. 431,736 9
Class No. 920/HAR
Caled. Classed
Prepared
Re-Bound... £4.95
INVOICE No. 39444

S/TRa IRe.

Printed and bound in Great Britain by R. J. Acford Ltd, Chichester, Sussex.

CONTENTS

ACKNOWLEDGEMENTS

The author gratefully acknowledges the help of: Mary Adams; Jill Allgood; Eamonn Andrews; Mary Baker; Frank Barker; Lady Isobel Barnett; Vivien and Paul Barnsley; Eric Bourne; Michael Barratt; Bernard Braden; Katie Boyle; G. H. Brook; Brian Clifford; Ken Curtis; Peter Cushing; Robin Day; Eric Dehn; André Deutsch, publishers of *Gilbert Harding by His Friends*; Midge Embery; John Faint; Arthur Godfrey; Joyce Grenfell; Charles Hamblett; Raymond Harris; Sam Heppner; Bill Hogg; Jack House; Fielden Hughes; Penelope Keith; Dicky Leeman; Library of the BBC; Library of the *Sunday People*; Joan McInnes; Brian Masters; Alan Melville; Ian Messiter; Norman A. L. Miller; John Montgomery; Matthew Newgate; David Nixon; Michael Noakes; Ewald Osers; Drucilla Pederson; John Pollard; Gil Purcell; Putnam & Co Ltd., publishers of *Along My Line*; Stanislau Quan; *Richmond & Twickenham Times*; Robin Russell; Madeleine Scott; Ray Seaton; Ronald Seth; Tom Sloan; Joan Smith; Roger Storey; *Sunday Times*; Muriel Sylvester; Charles Taylor; Bill Thomson; Leslie Tinkler; Sean Treacy; Patricia Warwick; Vera Watson; Mrs. P. H. White; Anona Winn; Sally Wright.

The illustrations are courtesy BBC Picture Library and Paul Popper Ltd.

CHAPTER 1

'A FREAK AT A SIDESHOW'

In his book *The Fifties* John Montgomery wrote: 'There was one man in Britain whose name was more widely known than that of the Prime Minister or any scientist or public figure. This was Gilbert Harding, regarded by radio listeners and television viewers as the rudest and worst tempered but still the most likeable personality in the country.'

Those who lived through the 1950s probably do not now remember, without prompting, many of the people and things that came and went in that decade. Brumas, Sabrina, Davy Crockett and Philip Harben ... 'winkle-pickers', stiletto heels and dirndl skirts ... *The Groves, The Huggetts* and *Educating Archie* ... Sylvia Peters and Mary Malcolm ... Denis Lotis, Pat Boone and Patti Page ... *Beat the Clock* and hula hoops ... Professor Joad and Commander Campbell ...

Gilbert Harding, however, still stays vividly in the mind, even with those whom one would have thought too young today to have been conscious of him in their extreme youth. This instant reaction to his name is doubtless because he was an original – the first ever 'TV personality'.

His appeal to the public was most certainly not based on looks. Bespectacled, with an old-fashioned moustache, he was rotund and patently middle-aged. He was always staid in his dress, by day in a business suit that made him look like a bank manager, and for evening performance the then BBC-prescribed dinner jacket, which he wore with all the flair of a suburban cinema manager.

It was necessary to invent the term 'TV personality' for him, since he fitted into no known category, had no conventional talent or training to entertain. He was not an actor, singer, comedian, musician, not a trained commentator like Raymond Glendenning, not an experienced interviewer like Robin Day. He appeared on television without re-hearsal, for there was nothing to rehearse. He was merely himself.

What was the secret of Gilbert Harding's tremendous popularity? How was he able, through his appearances on *What's My Line?* and his other programmes, to command an audience of eleven million? He was outrageous, insulting and unpredictable. He was also a witty, vulnerable and irresistable character, the victims of whose slashing tongue generally deserved their fate.

The strain of acting as curator for this unusual national monument often looked as if it would prove too much for the BBC. But they recognized his immense skill in using the media – first radio and later television. They realized that they had a hot property even if it was likely to blow up in their faces every now and then. All the same, one wonders how long an individualistic and eccentric career that so well caught the mood of the moment could have continued had it not been for his death in 1960. As one producer put it: 'A time came when we at the BBC began to wonder how much longer we could go on displaying this drunken homosexual, like a freak at a sideshow'.

CHAPTER 2

CANADIAN INTERLUDE

I first met Gilbert Harding immediately after the war in Toronto, where he was assistant to the BBC's representative at the Canadian Broadcasting Corporation's headquarters. His duties included arranging the Canadian link in world-wide hook-ups for *Family Favourites*.

Toronto at that time was a big city with a small town mentality. (Now it has changed; now it is a much bigger city.) Not without sound reason was it called 'Toronto the Good'. The city fathers, drawing to the full on their staunch Presbyterian background, appeared to operate solely on the basis of 'If it's fun, let's legislate against it.' Sunday papers were not allowed, there were no Sunday cinemas or pubs. In fact there were no pubs at any time, only 'beverage rooms' in which only beer was allowed; no spirits, no food, no entertainment. There was not a single restaurant worthy of the name, no nightclubs or downtown nightlife of any sort. Torontonians were legislated into having a real drink and making what entertainment they could in their own homes.

For the newcomer to Toronto it was a lonely, unfriendly city. Without anywhere to meet people, one could have a miserable time during the lengthy wait to get on to the 'party circuit', i.e. until one was invited to the parties that went on in the widely-scattered surburban homes. For the spectacularly convivial Gilbert Harding it was agony.

He had taken a place on Jarvis Street and when informed loftily by a Toronto matron, 'Jarvis Street is a bad address', he had replied: 'Madam *Toronto* is a bad address.' When he did get on to the party circuit he was to become very much in demand. In small-time cities such as Toronto there is always a nucleus of people who want to break away from the routine of husbands talking business and the lowering of the golf handicap, and wives talking domesticity and the problems of Spock-marked children. Harding joined the Toronto set which was interested in things more mentally stimulating and 'We must have Gilbert' became the by-word of the party givers of this coterie. He could always be relied upon to give good measure in intellectual argument and, if roused by any strait-laced Torontonian who might have drifted into the fold, he

3

would undoubtedly display what was later to be described as his 'talent to insult'.

His wit was instant and often as not caustic. He never gave any thought to people present whose feelings might be hurt. I remember being with him among a group of people when some woman's name was mentioned. 'Not only has she got a moustache,' he said, 'but she's got dandruff in it.'

He had a fund of anecdotes and the stories he told were frequently not just passed-on jokes but were perfectly true, as with his story of going down to New York and getting involved in the wartime shortage of hotel accommodation. Quentin Reynolds, the American war correspondent who had made a name for himself in Britain with his satirical broadcasts about Goebbels and Hitler, came to his rescue by inviting him to share his hotel room. Returning to the hotel one afternoon Harding found him deeply engaged in what Harding called 'horizontal refreshment' with a Hollywood starlet. Reynolds got out of bed and standing there naked he indicated the young lady and said: 'Gilbert, I don't believe you've met my sister.'

It was prior to this New York trip that Harding originated a quip which at least two well known television entertainers have since regaled as their own. Before he could go to New York he had to get a U.S. visa at the American consulate in Toronto. He was called upon to fill in a long form with many questions, including 'Is it your intention to overthrow the Government of the United States by force?' By the time Harding got to that one he was so irritated that he answered: 'Sole purpose of visit.'

None of us who knew Harding in the late 1940s in Toronto had any way of knowing that this lowly BBC employee was to become one of the most famous men in Britain. Even if he had never achieved his ultimate public reputation he would have remained for us an unforgettable character. Embraced by what might be termed the Toronto intelligentsia, he most certainly did not endear himself to the generality of conformist Torontonians. He was far too outspoken for them, and he in turn found them provincial and smug. Asked to address the Toronto Junior Chamber of Commerce, he got up, surveyed the gathering, remarked: 'No shirt too young to stuff', and sat down again.

The society matrons of Toronto and elsewhere in Canada were a particular target for him. At a dinner party when one of them, getting little response from him, asked, 'Would you prefer me to talk to the gentlemen on my left?' his reply was 'Infinitely.'

Their overdressing appalled him – 'Here she comes all dressed up like a well kept grave' – and he could not abide their insistence on their menfolk being similarly overdressed – tails for an evening of dancing at the rendezvous of the elite the Granite Club, dinner jackets for cocktail parties. Bernard Braden recalls being in his office when one of Toronto's socialites phoned him: '. . . Drinks at your home on Friday the seventeenth? I should be delighted, madam . . . Between six and eight p.m.? Yes, indeed . . . Black tie? I have a black tie but I don't think it would go well with the blue suit I'll be wearing . . . Oh, well, perhaps some other time, on some less important occasion . . . farewell, dear lady.'

On a visit to Vancouver he found that his ability to enliven any party had penetrated to that city and one of the front-runners of the Vancouver social whirl phoned to invite him to a dinner party. She would not listen to his efforts to get out of it; one of her cars would be sent to pick him up. In the chauffeur driven, pale fudge Cadillac on the way to the lady's mansion – described by Harding as 'in the later Greco-Japanese style' – the chauffeur asked him when he would like to be driven back to his hotel. 'On arrival,' said Harding.

A Toronto matron, having been the butt of one of his sallies and intent on scoring off him, said loudly enough for all present to hear, 'Tell me, Mr Harding, why aren't you in the war?' He replied: 'I have a physical disability, madam. No guts.' In truth, of course, he was unwanted at any recruiting office. He had chronic bronchitis and asthma necessitated an oxygen 'puffer' always being close at hand; without his glasses life was a blur.

Once he met someone ruder than he. He was a lecturer in psychology at Toronto University and at a small party Harding gave in his flat the man was so insulting that before long all the other guests had departed, and Harding was left alone with the professor. Helping himself liberally to some more of his host's liquor, the professor proceeded to tell Harding that at the art of insulting he was a beginner.

'Your weakness is that having insulted somebody, you turn soft,' he said. 'You apologise afterwards. You phone or send flowers in apology for your behaviour. When I insult somebody, they stay insulted.'

'That's interesting,' said Harding. 'I had not thought of it in that way. And now, sir, I wonder whether you would have the good grace to piss off.'

His bluntness was to get him into trouble with the police. A reason he lived on Jarvis Street was that it was the odd choice of location for the CBC head office, where he and his BBC boss had their little cubby-hole; odd because it was indeed a bad address in the eyes of local citizens. To them it was the city's 'red light district', even if that merely meant frequent comings and goings of taxis at old brownstone houses there. Nevertheless, police on patrol in the district went in pairs, which was to land Harding in hot water.

At an office party at the CBC one evening they ran out of ginger ale and since the Canadian national tipple, rye whisky, is undrinkable without it, Harding volunteered to go out and get some more Canada Dry. Weaving his far from steady way back from the drugstore with a quart bottle under each arm he passed two cops standing in a doorway. It so happened that at this time the papers were full of the story of police gunning down a youngster running away from robbing a candy store. As Harding staggered past the doorway the cops came out to enquire: 'Hey, bud, what do you think you're doing?' He turned and said: 'Oh, go off and shoot some more children.' At the party they waited for their ginger ale, wondering what had become of Gilbert ... and learned next day that he had spent the night in a police cell.

At another time he was taking a walk through Rosedale, where the 'better' people of Toronto lived, and came upon a dog running loose. He restored it to the householder, who slammed the door in his face without thanking him. Naturally he could not overlook such bad manners and the upshot was that the man called the police. A 'prowl car' took him downtown, where he was booked – or was supposed to be. He drew upon his experience as a policeman in Bradford to point out to the desk sergeant that he was charging him incorrectly. 'Okay,' said the sergeant, 'just get out.'

'Oh, no,' said Harding. 'I will not be put to the expense of getting a taxi to return to Rosedale, where I was enjoying a most pleasant stroll. One of your cars will drive me back to the place at which I was apprehended.'

'None available.'

'One will be made available.'

And sure enough he was driven back to Rosedale in a police car.

The reputation of the eccentric Englishman soon spread among people of all walks of life. Tom Sloan, who was to rise to high places within the BBC, tells of being on a trip to Canada and when he came out of the Royal York Hotel in Toronto and got into a taxi the driver, hearing his English accent, asked: 'Do you know a guy named Gilbert Harding?' It was logical that local taxi drivers were to get to know him, for throughout his grown-up life there was to be a close bond between him and taxi drivers – called upon on so many occasions to deliver Harding in his cups from his place of drinking to his lodgings.

Besides his fondness for a drink there was another aspect of the Harding make-up which some Torontonians had a hint of. Bill Hogg, who worked at that time at the CBC, tells of another office party there at which he came upon Gilbert Harding looking very dejected.

'What's wrong?'

'Graham's upset me.'

6

'What did he do?'

'Oh, nothing.'

'Was it something he said?'

'He's been mean to me.'

'In what way?'

'Oh, it's all right. Forget about it.'

Graham was an office boy.

That certainly started tongues wagging at the party. You can be *annoyed* by an office boy but you can't be *upset* by one. Unless, of course . . . Was Gilbert Harding one of Those . . . ?

In 1947 when it became known that the BBC were transferring him back to London, a Toronto public relations man who did not take kindly to Harding's term for a PRO – a 'presstitute' – said to him: 'I hear you're going back to England.' Harding nodded. 'Well.' the other went on, 'all I can say is that Canada's loss is England's loss.'

It also happened that shortly after Harding's departure I also returned to England and one day I bumped into him coming out of Broadcasting House. He looked unhappy and told me that the BBC had just unloaded him, could I do anything to help him get a job?

He felt hurt that: 'my old pals Stewart MacPherson, Dimbleby, Wynford Vaughan Thomas and Raymond Glendenning were now famous, while I was languishing in Canadian obscurity.' He said he would have to pick up what assignments he could. 'I can tell you,' he added, 'I do not relish having to join the out-of-work actors and BBC rejects hanging around the Broadcasting House pubs trying to get something out of the producers.' And later, in explanation of why the Corporation had fired him, he was to write: 'The BBC felt that I was not suited to the strictures of policy as it applied to staff and I was told to leave and freelance. I felt a little as though I had been thrown out of an aeroplane without a parachute . . . .'

CHAPTER 3

THE BOY FROM THE WORKHOUSE

Gilbert Charles Harding was born on June 5 1907 in the Dickensian atmosphere of a workhouse. His father and mother were Master and Matron of the Union Workhouse in Hereford, on a joint salary of £90 per annum.

The institution had formerly been run by his mother's parents, the Kings. Charles King had been a Buckinghamshire farm labourer before being employed in the Aylesbury Workhouse, where he did sufficiently well to be entrusted with the job of Master at Hereford. Their daughter May, who was to become Gilbert's mother, was born and grew up there.

Gilbert's grandparents on his father's side had lived in Caerleon-upon -Usk, near Newport, where his Grandfather Gilbert had charge of the Children's Home. His father, also Gilbert, was a Choral Scholar at Derby School and in the early 1900s came to the workhouse in Hereford to be assistant school master. It was thus that he and May King were brought together and married, and when the Kings retired from running the Union Workhouse they took over.

Christened Gilbert Charles for his father and maternal grandfather, he was to remember little of the former, since he died following an appendix operation in the winter of 1910-11 when Gilbert was only four. He had a vague remembrance of him getting the decorations and the festivities organised at the workhouse for the coronation of George V, which he did not live to enjoy.

Mr Harding had been a good footballer at club level and at cricket, according to the *Hereford Times* 'a fine bat and probably the best fast bowler in the county'. There is no doubt that had he lived beyond Gilbert's fourth birthday he would have had the boy out on the lawns of the workhouse teaching him how to swing a bat and dribble a soccer ball. Gilbert went without such fatherly influences. During his mature years, in explanation of his homosexuality, Gilbert told Vivien Barnsley, a friend of his sister: 'There were never enough men in my family life. I grew up surrounded by a mother, a sister, two maiden aunts, a grand-mother and – a grandfather whom I avoided by choice. There were so many women around me that the window cleaner used to wonder why I was always so glad to see him.'

When his father had died, that meant that Mrs Harding was out of a job since the general rule was that workhouses were run by a couple. Just turned 30, Mrs Harding had young Gilbert and his sister Constance, a year older, to bring up. However, fortunately for her but not for the inmates, who regarded him as a despot, Grandfather King was recalled from retirement to be Master again and she was allowed to stay on.

Mr King was described by John Pollard, who grew up with Gilbert, as 'a prim-faced, white-bearded Victorian'. Gilbert once wrote of him as 'a harsh, pompous, vain man'. He felt that Grandpa King's main aim as far as he was concerned was to make life miserable for him and he kept well out of his way. He sought instead the company of the inmates. An old lady named Mrs Cohen was normally housekeeper to an equally old but foul-tempered farmer and she would seek refuge in the workhouse until she felt she had enough strength to go back to him. She had the time, which his mother did not always have, to read to him by the hour. A one-legged man called Nick would keep him so enraptured with his yarns of his adventures during his years before the mast that Gilbert felt like one of the boys in the Millais painting *The Boyhood of Raleigh* and he still thought with pleasure and affection of old Nick even when he learned later that he had not only never been in sailing ships but had never even seen the sea. Gilbert found the inmates 'the kindliest of people'.

The Union Workhouse, called such because it was controlled by a union of parishes, was built in 1836 to accommodate 300, although at the time the Hardings ran it there were usually about 180 inmates. The buildings still exist, a two-storey complex with slate roof and including quite a large house which was for the Master and Matron, and a Chapel. In the later years of its original function it was renamed the Public Assistance Institution in an not entirely successful effort to remove the 'workhouse' stigma and then in 1937, with Queen Mary laying the foundation stone, it was incorporated into a hospital development scheme known as the County Hospital. The house of the Master and Matron, where Gilbert was born and brought up, now bears the legend 'The Nurses Administrative Offices'.

One is always tempted to speak of the 'Dickensian atmosphere' whenever a workhouse is mentioned, bearing in mind no doubt such things as the vividly depressing opening sequence of David Lean's film of *Oliver Twist*, when his unfortunate mother is giving birth to him in the squalor of a Victorian poorhouse. However, in the twentieth century and thanks in no small measure to the crusading of Dickens the scene was much changed.

9

The main part of the Union Workhouse was a not unattractive building with spick-and-span rooms and the extensive gardens were beautifully looked after, plenty of labour being available among the inmates for them to help the gardeners to keep them that way. Harding looked back fondly to his time spent growing up there – the trim lawns a profusion of flowers and flowering shrubs ('Each new season brought new wonders and colours to delight me,' he once wrote)... the abundance of gooseberries, raspberries, loganberries and mulberries for the picking... the market garden with 'wonderfully fresh' tomatoes, cucumbers and giant vegetable marrows. It was 'a small paradise' for a youngster to play in. 'My sister and I,' wrote Harding, 'were considered very lucky by local children. This was before we went to school, where the attitude to our workhouse background was one of resentment. But while we were master and mistress of the highly desirable workhouse gardens, children from the outside world would compete for the honour of being invited to play with us.'

When Harding became famous and well-off it was inevitable that a newspaper editor, at the appropriate time of the year, would ask him to do a feature on the lines of *It Was Christmas Day in the Workhouse*, although not of course sticking strictly to that famous poem's story line. Harding described how, from the year he was born, 1907, until 1922, when he moved with his mother and sister to Bradford, he spent every Christmas in the Hereford workhouse, 'called by those who thought the word offensive "the institution" and by those who did not think it offensive enough the "grubber" or the "spike".' Preparations began in September with his mother supervising the mixing of the Christmas puddings, which must have been of Mrs Beeton proportions, since *buckets* of beer and stout and a bottle or so of rum were poured into the mixture. 'Somehow,' in Gilbert's view, 'it always tasted better raw than when cooked.'

Christmas day began early. At 6 a.m. the workhouse launderers and nurses, augmented by a Miss Pugh, unidentified except as possessor of a beautiful voice, and two of her friends from the Hereford Cathedral choir, went around the hospital singing carols. The Guardians of the Poor had special grants to help with the financing of the day and this included Christmas treats – sweets and snuff for the old ladies, cigarettes and tobacco for the men and toys for the children. 'My sister and I went around helping to distribute these. I suppose it gave us some sense of being little benefactors.'

Mr Scrivens the baker cooked joints of beef, ham and pork in his huge bake ovens. Christmas dinner was served at 12.30. It was all very festive. The dining hall was brightly decorated and some of the

10

Guardians came to approve the pudding, followed by a glass of sherry or a nip of whisky with Gilbert's grandfather. The old cellarman, Dan Tomkins, broached the barrels and drew the ale. As a reward he was given a quart pewter mug of beer and the young Harding was always impressed as he watched old Dan, with the mug kept at his lips, down the whole quart in one go without any movement of his adam's apple. Then he would get down to serious drinking.

Mr Porlock, the local shoemaker, brought his gramophone, a crank-handle affair with a horn, and entertained the inmates while they had tea. Then there was an evening concert at which Alistair Proctor, of the cathedral choir, sang traditional Christmas songs and Miss Pugh sang *Come Into the Garden Maud*, *Somewhere a Voice is Calling* and *There's a Long, Long Trail Awinding*.

'Simple pleasures,' Harding reflected in this article in 1954. 'Now there are no workhouses, but instead rest centres and homes for the frail and elderly. I am sure it is better so but judging from the letters I get from poor old folks trying to live on the old age pension, many a Christmas would be happier if there were still benevolent institutions like the Guardians of the Poor.'

Mrs Annie Davies recalled that when she was a 'help' at the workhouse part of her duties had been to take Gilbert out in his pram and look after him during the toddler stage. She found him 'a very naughty and self-willed child, and even in his early years the affinity between him and his mother was very marked.'

Mrs Harding was the middle one of the three daughters of Grand-father King – Edith, May and Ethel – and the only one who married. Why did Edie and Ethel never marry? 'They were too old-fashioned to get married,' said Mrs Patricia Warwick, another who had been a 'help', in the King's home from 8.30 to 12 each morning for two shillings – reduced to 1s 3d if she had a piece of bread and dripping. 'They never went out to places where they could come in contact with men.' They acted like Victorian young ladies, which in fact they were, having been born in the late 1870s (Edie) and at the beginning of the 1880s (May and Ethel). Grandfather King was the typical Victorian paterfamilias, treating his three daughters like untalented Bronte sisters. So wedded was he to the Victorian image that he had modelled himself on the Queen's son Edward – in appearance, that is, not in regard to the high life and sexual excursions.

The three King girls had a cloistered life imposed upon them and the only one who staged a breakout was May, who had ambitions to make something of her life. The thing closest at hand to be ambitious about was the goal of being Matron at the Hereford Union Workhouse,

11

but there was a stumbling block. To be Matron one had to be married. How much love was there in her marriage to the workhouse school teacher Charles Harding? It was a question posed by those who were around at the time, perhaps unfairly. However, when her husband died she insisted that there be no tombstone above his grave; the ground should be levelled above his remains. She said: 'The body should be forgotten; the spirit needs no memorial.' Other members of the family were shocked.

When Mrs Harding had become Matron at the workhouse Edie was assistant matron, while Ethel stayed at the King home nursing the ailing Mrs King. Those who knew May Harding regarded her as a cut above the others. Although having to wear 'full' clothes to camouflage an incipient beam, she was always well dressed. 'She wore silk stockings when they were only just coming into fashion,' a friend commented. She never did any menial work. Her assistant matron, Edie, did. Edie was always to be seen in an apron over her old-fashioned Victorian clothes, which included high black buttoned boots and black stockings.

Mrs Harding had what those who knew her called a 'posh' accent, quite unlike anyone else in the family. Mrs Muriel Sylvester, whose parents had charge of the Children's Home attached to the workhouse, remembers that when Mrs Harding brought presents of chocolate to her and her sister it was not the everyday product of Messrs Cadbury, Rowntree or Fry but imported Swiss chocolate by Suchard, a name familiar in England now, but then very exotic indeed. In its small way it was a reflection of an aspect of her make-up which she was to pass on to Gilbert, or rather, which he was to copy out of devotion to her – good taste, allied to a certain amount of snobbery. Reflecting on his childhood at the workhouse, Harding wrote: 'There is something very peculiar – and quite damaging to the ego – about being brought up in a workhouse as the child of the Master and Matron. There are so many people around to wait on you and call you master Gilbert. You get the feeling you are somebody. When you get outside the workhouse and start growing up away from the environment, you find you are not some kind of princeling at all. Indeed, you learn that children of workhouse officials are regarded as little better than the pauper inmates.'

Having what he felt was that cross to bear was bad enough, but to go on from there to an orphanage school – he was doubly inviting scorn. Did the stigma of 'born in a workhouse and educated at an orphanage' have an effect on him as a grown person? Any psychiatrist would tell you that it could not help but be a contributing factor to the aggressive Gilbert Harding of the public image.

The Royal Orphanage, Wolverhampton had been founded in 1850 as the Wolverhampton Orphan Asylum to provide shelter and education for children orphaned in the cholera epidemic of 1848, and was to become recognised as a secondary school in 1920 and was then given permission by King George VI for the new name of the Royal Wolverhampton School in its centenary year in 1950. When Gilbert arrived there in 1916 it was housed in an imposing building off Penn Road, Wolverhampton, and harboured 220 boys and 130 girls.

Mrs Harding had with her an empty suitcase in which to take home the clothes he was wearing as a horse-drawn cab took them from the Low Level station to the Royal Orphanage. Being delivered to boarding school is not an easy time for any boy and this was perhaps more difficult than usual for the nine-year-old Gilbert being transplanted from the sheltered, pampered life behind the workhouse walls. He recalled: 'I was a very spoilt little boy, badly behaved, selfish and liable to fits of temper if I did not get my own way quickly enough. Now all I felt was the terrifying and almost unbelievable sense of leaving behind for ever the carefree days and the knowledge that I was going to be separated from my mother, who had been my protector and shield.'

Typically his mother was upset at the sight of him transferred into uniform and bringing his own clothes to her to take home and just as typically saying to him: 'I have seen your dinner and it looks very nice.'

The uniform, in Gilbert's view, would have upset anybody. Like that of Christ's Hospital, 'but falling far short of it', it consisted of blue coats and white bibs worn over moleskin breeches and brown stockings, and 'dreadful heavy boots, the very sight of which depressed me'. The girls wore 'hideous' blue tunics, stiff white collars and cuffs and 'unbelievably hideous' straw hats – not that the boys had opportunity to examine the girls' uniforms closely. Boys and girls were rigidly separated and even at one of the few common meeting grounds – chapel – to cast as much as a sidelong glance at the girls would bring a reprimand.

The Royal Orphanage boys' uniform left its scars. When he went on to university his main concern on arrival there and seeing all the old school ties was that someone would ask him where his was. There was no such thing at his school . . . and that awful word 'orphanage' would come out.

Another, more lasting, imprint the school left on him came when the headmaster, the Rev. Frank ('Dad') Lampitt, died during the term time and the senior boys were ushered into his room to see him 'laid out'. Although not known as such, Lampitt was at heart an Anglo-Catholic and the boys were surprised to see him dressed in what to them was strange clerical clothing. He wore the vestments of celebrants of Mass – the chasuble, stole and alb. The young Harding was fascinated by this early glimpse of Catholic drama, a fascination which was to obsess

13

him more and more as he grew older and which was one of the several main influences on his becoming a Roman Catholic convert.

Frank Barker, who went to school with Gilbert and now lives in Birmingham, wrote to me: 'I was nine years of age and he about 17 and, having been through the school's normal course, was staying on as a fee-paying student being coached for university entrance. Occasionally, perhaps through temporary absence of a teacher, he took charge of junior classes and on the slightest provocation – inability to answer a question properly or mis-pronunciation of a word – he would hand out severe punishment. He favoured the sharp edge of a ruler on the knuckles of a clenched fist, raising black blood blisters. It was not that we were an unruly lot; far from it, we were all cowed and only too anxious to avoid his attention. He simply enjoyed inflicting pain.

'One Sunday evening, not feeing too well and having been excused attendance at evening prayer in the school chapel, I was in bed when he came prowling round the dormitories. He sat on the edge of my bed and after enquiring what I was doing there put his hand under the bedclothes, pulled up my nightshirt and began pinching my bottom. He pulled and twisted the flesh, all the time grinning with tightly closed teeth. It was days before I could sit down in any comfort. Two or three days later in our communal weekly bath my school mates commented on the extensive bruises over the whole area of my bottom and upper thighs. They sympathised but none gave a thought, as neither did I, of reporting the matter to higher authority. It just wasn't done and Harding was one of the crosses we had to bear.

'At that age of course I didn't know the meaning of homosexuality but with hindsight my experience did have such undertones. As far as I know there were no similar incidents; the victim would in any case be so embarrassed by such attentions that he would keep it quiet and my experience only became known to fellow members of my form because of the evidence visible when bathing.'

Harding found that they were 'astonishingly well taught'. Although Lampitt's approach had been to din it into his pupils – learn everything by rote, parrot fashion – he had a good record of getting boys to Oxford. Gilbert was one of three who sat for the Fowler Scholarship to Cambridge, worth £250 a year, and was bitterly disappointed when he managed only to come second. He resigned himself to a 'redbrick' but his preparations for a Second Division university were happily interrupted by the news that the boy who had won had decided to pull out of Cambridge. Gratefully Gilbert always remembered his name – Philip Chavasse.

14

In the latter years of his life when he took a young student under his wing, giving him the run of his London flat and devoting much time to furthering him, Harding told him why he was doing so. 'I do not want you to make the same mistakes in life that I did. I wasted my time at Cambridge.'

He certainly did not pursue his studies with diligence. A great deal of his time was spent on the activities of the Cambridge Union. He aspired to be President but did not achieve it, so he settled for being a hard-working member of the committee, concerning himself very much with seeing to the well-being of distinguished guest-speakers, particularly in the hospitality room after the debates. Which, at a stroke, satisfied two facets of his character very much in evidence throughout his life – being impressed by important people and liking a drink.

Thus he was able to meet Sir Arthur Conan Doyle (good name-dropping material), but found him disappointingly obsessed with spiritualism during the committee room drinking session. Lord Citrine was more rewarding but was such a persuasive Labourite that Harding felt he 'should stop lazing by the Cam and go down and do some useful work in the docks by the Thames.'

When the guest speaker was to be the Earl of Birkenhead, who had won his fame as a lawyer as F. E. Smith, Gilbert was very much excited, not only at the prospect of rubbing shoulders with a man of such stature but because Law was something which greatly interested him (he himself was to study for the Bar). He knew the famous F. E. Smith cases, including the story which could well have been true of his acting for an industrial firm being sued for compensation by a young man who claimed that he had lost the use of his right arm through an accident for which they were culpable. When the man, with his arm hanging stiffly at his side, was being questioned in court F. E. Smith asked him:

'Will you show the court how far you can lift your right arm?'

The youth, with great effort, managed to raise it only a short distance from his body.

'I see,' said Smith. 'Now tell me, how far could you raise it before the accident?'

'Oh, right up here,' said the young man, raising it above his head.

Case dismissed.

Gilbert had done his homework about Lord Birkenhead to the extent of knowing that his favourite tipple was brandy and with the good taste and sense of rightness inherited from his mother he departed from the usual whisky-and-sandwiches on this occasion and dipped into committee funds not only to provide the best Napoleon brandy but also to buy the correct glasses in which to serve it. He was pleased that Birkenhead, on asking who had furnished the brandy and being told it was one

15

Gilbert Harding, said to him: 'Splendid perception. You deserve to go far in life.' But this did not prevent Gilbert from coming to the conclusion that he was a 'monumentally arrogant man', a verdict which may have stemmed to a degree from his pique at the fact that, as he told his sister afterwards, 'I'd been looking forward to getting into that brandy but F. E. hogged it and there wasn't much for the rest of us.'

What he regarded as one of his happiest encounters was with G. K. Chesterton, who came to speak at a Union debate and adopted Harding as 'a sort of mascot'. The huge man – nicknamed 'Chest-a-ton' – was very kind to him during his stay in Cambridge, as well as for many years afterwards. 'This first time we talked together he told me I was far too nervous and much too lacking in self-confidence. It amused Gilbert Keith Chesterton to call me Gilbert the Less, flatteringly assuring me that he was referring only to my physical size.'

Chesterton was a spectacular figure at the time, his great bulk flamboyantly set off by broad-brimmed hat and green-lined cloak. Some time after this first meeting, Gilbert the Less felt prompted to ape him and acquired a cloak and slouch hat. The cloak was in fact a nurse's cloak, from which he removed the red flannel lining and had a green one stitched in, and the whole effect he confessed made him look like a replica of the well known advertisement for Sandeman's Port. However, he persisted, but without gaining the reputation for eccentricity and aestheticism he had hoped for. After several weeks of parading the streets with his cloak and hat brim flapping in the breeze, he felt hurt that nobody paid the slightest attention to him. He abandoned the venture and switched to affecting a cloth cap. This brought happier results. Someone came up to him and asked whether he was Sean O'Casey.

Shortly after this his mother was paying him a visit at Cambridge when someone who knew him well told her he thought her son had many childlike qualities. Having just emerged from one of their not infrequent head-on collisions, his mother snapped: 'One can hardly call them qualities and they are certainly not child*like*. To my mind they are child*ish*.'

At Cambridge he got involved in the usual japes of the type which gave rise to the term 'undergraduate humour'. He and some of his companions at Queens' went to a musical comedy that was playing at the New Theatre, each armed with a piece of calico. As was usual in such entertainments in those days there was a high-kicking chorus line and each time the legs went up the young men would tear a strip off the calico. The manager had them thrown out.

On another occasion there was someone of their age group who served in an antique shop who made it plain that he did not like university students and Harding and friends were only too pleased to dislike him reciprocally. One day they went into the shop and one of them took a large black chamber pot, decorated with a design of red roses, and having thrust it under his gown he made off with it out of the shop. The young man gave chase and when Harding's friend felt he had got far enough away from the shop to make it interesting, he let himself be caught and the young man retrieved the chamber pot. The students had specially chosen a hot day for their escapade. The shop assistant was in his shirtsleeves, had nowhere to hide the jerry and had to walk through the crowded streets carrying it for all to see. Gilbert and his friends enjoyed the spectacle.

In contrast to these frivolities a more serious side to his character was also developing. Having first become inclined towards Roman Catholicism at the sight of the raiments of his headmaster at school in Wolverhampton, Gilbert now came under two other influences which were to play their part in his eventually deciding definitely to become a convert. One was his supervising tutor, Laffan, and the other was the man who had taken such a kindly interest in him when he had come as a guest speaker to the Cambridge Union. Harding wrote:

Towards the end of my stay at the university, G.K. Chesterton invited me to lunch with him in Soho. I put off going to Bradford to see my mother in order to keep this date with my mentor. We went to a restaurant in Charlotte Street where, with his usual zest for doing things well, he tried to teach me how to eat spaghetti. We laughed uproariously at my awkwardness ... G.K.'s laughter was always kindly.

On my mentioning that, but for his invitation, I would have been in Bradford, he asked whether I knew the Rev. John O'Connor. I did indeed know him, having met him some months earlier while on holiday. This I told Chesterton, adding that I had been greatly impressed by O'Connor's wonderful personality. Only then did Chesterton tell me that my new Bradford friend was the original Father Brown, the Roman Catholic priest whose hobby was criminology, and hero of Chesterton's The Wisdom of Father Brown *and the other books.*

Chesterton suddenly went on to say: 'You, my boy, will inevitably become a Roman Catholic, too.'

In spite of his worries about his workhouse-orphanage background on arrival at Cambridge, it did not cause any concern to his companions there, several of whom were to become life-long friends. But it still weighed heavily upon the sensitive, easily hurt Gilbert and he was to write:

Despite the wonderful breakfast parties and club dinners, I had never

17

been able to afford to go to any of the college balls held in 'May Week',
which as everyone knows lasts a fortnight and takes place at Cambridge
in June. It is that festive time when parents and sisters and eligible
girl cousins come to enjoy the end-of-academic-year 'bust up' and have
fun in general.

My college, with its tradition of non-extravagance, only held a May
Ball every three years, and I longed to attend it. But I knew there were
lean days ahead; my £250 scholarship would shortly come to an end.
I felt I could no longer live on my mother's hard-earned money. So as
May Week approached I watched the great marquees going up on
the college lawns and saw the gay illuminations being hung up over the
bridges and by the banks of the river, and I prayed for a miracle to
happen to bring me the wherewithal to go to a ball in style.

The miracle did not happen. I could not afford the seven guineas
for a double ticket, and I refused to slink in on my own and be a mere
bystander. I would have needed several more guineas to pay my whack
at the champagne buffet. Altogether the notion that I, a prospective
clergyman, should so desperately long to attend these revels was absurd.

So I said nothing to anyone, and managed on the whole to excuse
myself from those invitations which I did receive. One night, however,
as I was cycling back to Queens' from some fairly dreary meeting, I
looked across the river and stopped pedalling. Against the incomparable
backcloth of the great Chapel and Gibbs' Building was the King's
May Ball in full swing.

Leaning on my bicycle handlebars, I heard the seductive music, saw
the flash of beautiful girls in lovely dresses, watched slim young men in
white ties and tails escort their partners to punts moored beside the lawn,
and I felt very sorry for myself. There was only a narrow stretch of
river between me and the scene. As I listened to the happy laughter
and heard the gay click of champagne glasses, it made me feel very much
indeed that I was a 'have not'.

He had entered Cambridge to read Modern Languages – French and
German – but his supervisors had soon given up trying to make him
work diligently at these subjects and he had abandoned them for the
supposedly less taxing History and was thus able to enjoy to the full
his Union activities, his japes, bathing at Byron's Pool and breakfasts
and sherry parties at his and other people's rooms.

There was the necessity, however, of knuckling down to his final
exam and he was fortunate in this regard in having as a close friend
John Leathem, who was to go on to be headmaster of Taunton School.
The paper was on ancient history and when he confessed to Leathem
that it was something about which he knew practically nothing, his

friend said flippantly, 'Oh that's all right. All you need to know is about Draco, the City States and the Peloponnesian War.'

Overjoyed when he found that three of the questions were indeed on those topics, he answered those questions and those only and scraped through with a Third Class Honours Degree in History.

CHAPTER 4

THE WANDERING CATHOLIC

On coming down from Cambridge in 1928 Gilbert Harding embarked on the first step towards his chosen rôle in life, to become an Anglican minister. As preparation for his ordination he went to the Community of the Resurrection at Mirfield, near Huddersfield. An advantage of this choice was that he was only some fifteen miles from his mother in Bradford. She had gone there in 1922 to take up a post with the Bowling Park institution for the poor, when the retirement of Grandfather King from the Hereford workhouse had meant that she also had to go.

Gilbert's time in a cassock among the clerics at Mirfield was short-lived. Being required to observe each night the Great Silence and having a text rather pointedly hung over his bed which read 'I will give heed unto my ways and offend not with my tongue' was hardly his scene. With the lack of singleness of purpose which was to plague him until someone decided for him that broadcasting was his *métier*, he abandoned his ambition to become a minister and salvaged what he could from his months of being ordinand. 'After all,' he reasoned, 'I have been taught theology so well at Mirfield that I should take their Anglo-Catholic teachings to their logical conclusion and become a Roman Catholic.'

The four men who were the chief influences in his becoming a convert were, as mentioned, 'Dad' Lampitt, his tutor Laffan and G. K. Chesterton, with the addition of William Wright – 'Father Billy' – a priest with whom he had made friends and who was as wretchedly poor as his parishioners in a Sunderland slum. He was a man so dedicated that he gave his flannel trousers to someone with nothing to wear, and was going around in his football shorts under his cassock until Harding provided him with a replacement.

The lapsed Anglican went back to his home territory of Hereford to the Benedictine Abbey of St Michael and All Souls at Belmont on the outskirts of the town. There he was initiated into the rituals and doctrines which formed his basic fascination with the Church of Rome – the seven sacraments, transubstantiation, the sacrificial aspect of the Mass, purgatory, the infallibility of the Pope and the immaculate conception of the Virgin Mary. On June 29, 1929, on the Feast of St Peter and St Paul, he became a Roman Catholic.

Did conversion to the Roman Catholic church *help* Gilbert Harding, especially in regard to his worries about his way of life?

It had no effect on his drinking. If he had abandoned the Anglican church to become a Methodist or a Baptist he would have had to abandon the bottle also; if he had turned to Presbyterianism he would have been given a conscience about drink. But in the Catholic church he was on safe ground. The Church of Rome does not disallow alcohol. If it did it would be in danger of losing, *en masse*, an important group of its staunchest adherents – the Southern Irish.

As to his homosexuality, he has gone on record as saying that he did not find the Catholic church particularly helpful. Fielden Hughes, who is now a travel consultant, was chairman of the radio programme *Say the Word*, on which Gilbert Harding was a frequent guest, and he recalled that once he confided in him: 'I've spent vast sums with psychiatrists trying to get rid of this tendency. And the time I've spent with priests in confession! Do you know all the priests could say to me? "Control yourself." Now what sort of guidance is that – "control yourself!" '

In the autumn of 1977 the BBC put out on radio a discussion programme on this matter of the Church and its attitude towards homosexuality. Most of those taking part were Anglican ministers and Roman Catholic priests, several of them confessed homosexuals. The dilemma of the Church, as they expressed it, was that it must take cognizance of the fact that more than two million people in Britain were in that category. It was realised that you cannot 'cure' a person of being homosexual. So the attitude of the Church at this time appeared to be to advise celibacy, the clerics on the programme putting it in this succinct way: 'Be it, but don't do it.' Which would seem to have been the line of thought encountered by Harding among priests during confession.

Harding liked to say 'As is usual with converts, I am more Catholic than the Pope himself'. But just how ardent was Gilbert? In a reminiscence he wrote in 1953 he said: 'After my conversion in 1929, on becoming better acquainted with it, I found the Roman Catholic ritual in many ways less splendid than that of the Anglo-Catholic faith. I had fits of argument about the relics and indulgences, which I always found difficult to believe in.' Such doubts persisted and in his mature life he used to have violent arguments with Father Christie at the Farm Street Church in Mayfair, which was known as the fashionable church for Roman Catholics in London and as such naturally had an attraction for Gilbert.

Initially he had been full of enthusiasm. He told Christopher Sykes: 'To me the Church is an adorable new mother, but to you she is your old aunt.' Later in life he admitted to Frank Singleton: 'My practice is deplorable but I always like to have a tame priest on hand. Confession, you know . . .'

As to his practice of the faith, there were times when he would go for a rather lengthy period without a visit to church and Alan Melville, his friend and neighbour in Brighton, relates:

'One day I was going off to play tennis and on the way to the courts I bumped into Gilbert. He was looking very earnest and I asked him where he was going. "The time has come, dear boy," he said, "for me to be re-embraced into the arms of Rome. I have fallen from grace. I have . . ." And then he went on to enumerate all the ways in which he felt he had fallen by the wayside. He was going to confess all to the priest.

'It so happened that we had barely got our game of tennis started than it began raining. Soon it was pelting down, so we went off to a pub. Much to my surprise who should I see at the far end of the bar but Gilbert, well into the liquid refreshment. I went over to him.

"That didn't take long." I said.

'Gilbert's reply was: "I said to the priest that I had been drinking too much, I had failed regular attendance at Mass, I had committed this sin and that sin. "Why?" the priest asked. "Mind your own business, you little pipsqueak," I said, and here I am back on it." '

However, the Catholic blood he now felt he possessed rose in him when residence in Brighton made him aware of the activities each November 5 of the Bonfire Society of Lewes, the nearby county town. Members of the Society would, and still do, burn an effigy of the Pope in memory of the Lewes Martyrs, who suffered at the hands of the Catholics many years ago. Harding wrote a letter to the *Brighton Evening Argus* branding this 'gross insult to the Pope' as 'disgraceful' and he started a campaign to have the Society's Guy Fawkes Day ceremony stopped. The campaign was hardly successful. On the following November 5 the Bonfire Society set alight *two* effigies – one of the Pope and one of Gilbert Harding. Gilbert was deeply hurt.

He did not let conversion to the Roman Catholic church affect his work, as it did with such converts as Evelyn Waugh and, more particularly, Graham Greene, whose perception as a writer has often been clouded by his apparent necessity to insinuate Catholic propaganda into his novels.

And anyone who knew Gilbert well never had Catholicism inflicted upon them by him. It was his own problem.

Having in 1929 become a Catholic and reached the age of 22, he then had to find a job. His Cambridge tutor Laffan gave him a letter of introduction to a City of London firm which was seeking merchant apprentices for their business houses in Singapore and Shanghai. Nothing came of that. Then, oddly enough, he was interested in the prospects of taking an executive post in a canning factory. Those who interviewed him for the job decided, perhaps wisely, that he was not quite the right type for them. So he became what he had vowed he never would become – a teacher.

The Abbot of Belmont offered him the position of lay schoolmaster at the Abbey. Acknowledging himself to be 'restless, argumentative and gregarious', he did not find it easy to adjust to life in a monastery, even though a layman among the monks and therefore not bound by their routine. He got into arguments about dogma; he would come home from having a convivial time with old Hereford friends and have to run the gauntlet of the disapproving stares of the monks, 'fifty grave and tonsured men', lining up to go into Compline, the last evening service.

On annual pay of merely £75, all found, he was still plagued by his Cambridge debts but one very pleasing outcome of being at Belmont Abbey was that when he confessed his debts to a Father John Owen, the priest asked him to hand over all his bills to him. In a matter of a few days they were returned to him, receipted. He was told that they had been paid by an 'unknown Catholic of means'. It was a relief to have that off his mind, even though he had been so ashamed of how much he owed that he had not given Father Owen all his bills. Years later when he had become famous he was to learn that although Cambridge (and Oxford) tradesmen 'were only too glad to let gentlemen of the University have unlimited credit', they had something in common with income tax inspectors. They had long memories. One day in 1953, precisely a quarter of a century after he had left the university, he was in Cambridge to do a radio programme and dropped in to the tobacco shop of Messrs Ora, in Trinity Street, to buy some cigarettes. As he was about to pay for them a courteous gentleman behind the counter said: 'By the way, Mr Harding, we have a small account on our books, which is of course statute barred, but perhaps you might care to settle it now.'

When he wrote in his reminiscences of his time at Belmont Abbey, he concluded: 'After an unsatisfactory year at Belmont I thought I needed a change.' Three terms at a school would seem to be a short period for a teacher to decide he should move on – unless there was some special reason for the decision.

I have received a letter from Stanislaus Quan: 'In response to an advertisement in *The Universe* I went to Belmont Abbey, Hereford, in

August 1929 and met the Headmaster, Father Anselm Lightbound, O.S.B. (later an Abbot). It was then a small boarding school with about 50-60 boys, ranging from about 7 to 15-16. Now, of course, it is a Roman Catholic public school in the Headmasters' Conference, with five times that many pupils. In 1929 I was told I would have to teach almost everything, save maths and Greek. About a month later I was offered the job and I remained on the staff until 1939 . . .

'I was often asked to take evening study periods when Father Anselm had an unexpected "call". This I always took to be for the sick and the dying, and I did this willingly, until I discovered that the frequent "calls" were for games of bridge in Hereford . . .

'One of the first things I learned on arrival at the school was that the previous resident teacher had been a man called Gilbert Harding and that he had been asked to leave because of some trouble or other with the boys (all boarders). What this trouble was I did not inquire and I did not know at the time. I ought to mention that in those early days I was quite ignorant of anything homosexual, and so gossip about things of that nature largely passed me by. My wife is a Herefordian, daughter of a well-known businessman in Hereford and a benefactor of Belmont Abbey. She told me subsequently that Gilbert Harding used to take boys down to the river (the monks had a right-of-way down to the Wye to their own landing stage for boating) and that this caused the problem.

'A year or two later, Gilbert Harding visited the Abbey. I was introduced to him and together we went down to Hereford. I have completely forgotten where we went or when we parted. All I vividly remember was that when we had got outside the Abbey drive on to what is known as the New Road, linking the Abbey grounds to the main Hereford road, he quite casually – as if he was used to that sort of thing – undid his trousers and as we walked along he piddled down the middle of the road. As I wasn't used to such behaviour I was quietly embarrassed, but I concluded that that was what people do, and fortunately no one was about, so I thought no more about it.

'Many years later – in the late 1950s – I was in the Mitre Hotel in Broad Street, Hereford, (now the National Westminster Bank) having a drink after an evening lecture. It was very near 10 p.m. and closing time. Gilbert Harding, then a national figure, came in, leant against the long curved bar, and complained in a loud voice about the impossibility of getting a proper meal at that hour. He was eventually supplied with sandwiches. He did not recognise me, seated in a corner with a book and a Guinness. I can see him now, leaning against the bar with a large bulbous glass of brandy in his hand, his face turned up as if addressing someone over the top of the bar. Gilbert Harding's voice was quite exceptional – it was arresting, cultured and clear. There was nothing affected about it, because it was natural to him, and this quality came out in his TV programmes.'

After Harding left Belmont Abbey in 1929, he was a teacher (briefly) at a prep. school in Tonbridge, Kent. Then he went back to the Benedictines, this time to the monks of Fort Augustus in Scotland who ran a school beautifully situated on the shores of a loch. The school still functions and one can see the boys setting off in their rowboats from the boating sheds in high hope of seeing the Loch Ness monster, since Fort Augustus is at the southern end of that much publicised stretch of water. After a brief stay there, the Wandering Catholic taught (briefly) at a prep. school monks had just opened in Edinburgh.

That year, 1931, he met the Rector of a Canadian university who had come to Britain seeking staff and he was soon on a ship for Nova Scotia, to be Professor of English at the Catholic St Francis Xavier College in Antigonish, deep in the hinterland of Halifax.

Two memories of his (brief) stay there remained imprinted on his mind. One was that his French-Canadian students, having had antagonism towards Englishness in any form instilled into them by their parents from birth, were aggressively uninterested in learning English. And the other lasting memory was the difficulty in finding a place to drink. Worse than that: having found such a place, being required by law – as he discovered some years later in Ontario and elsewhere in Canada – to consume your drink only while sitting down, in the bleak surroundings of a 'beverage room', with no decorations, no food, no music or any other type of amenity. Once, in desperation, he made a 200 mile round trip from Antigonish to New Glasgow to find such a location in which to down a few pints.

Drink played such a dominant part in his life when he became a public figure that many felt that keeping up the pace of the radio-TV ratrace had driven him to it. He fostered this idea by saying: 'I drink too much because I'm tired, and I'm tired because I drink too much.' But his fondness for a drink was with him from his earliest days. He met his needs at Antigonish when he learned that liquor restrictions in Canada were less strict if one purchased by the bottle and he kept a very well stocked cupboard in his room.

When we knew Gilbert in the latter part of the 1940s in Toronto he offered my wife an explanation for his drinking. She was having a drink with him on the terrace of the Toronto Yacht Club when right out of the blue he said to her: 'You're pregnant.'

'How do you know?' she said. 'My husband doesn't even know yet.'

'I can tell by your eyes.'

'Oh, nonsense. You've had too much to drink.'

'Do you think I drink too much ?'

'Well . . .'

'I am sure you do,' said Gilbert, 'but there's a perfectly good explanation. When my mother was pregnant my Aunt Edie came around to see her one evening and was told she was down at the local. When Edie went there she found my mother well and truly into the gin. "I do believe you're trying to get rid of it." said Edie. It was that popular old wives' tale that a liberal quantity of gin and a boiling hot bath would do the trick. My mother confessed that that was the case. She had four more before they left. So it isn't surprising, is it, that I have a liking for a drink, considering that when I was a mere foetus I was swilling around in all that gin ?'

Perhaps nearer the mark would be to borrow from Alan Brien a turn of phrase and to say that to Gilbert Harding words were alcohol but the trouble was, so was alcohol. He was certainly not an alcoholic. For one thing, he loved eating and got much pleasure from good food; the alcoholic's idea of a substantial meal is to add milk to what he is drinking. Unlike the cheerless determination of the alcoholic to pour liquor into himself, Harding *enjoyed* his drink. It stimulated him, put his mind in top gear, just as it did a famous contemporary of his. Those who had known Winston Churchill well would be able to say how often *his* intake of alcohol exceeded the required amount to sharpen his already keen mind. In Harding's case there were three phrases to his drinking, at a party, in the pub. Phase one: slightly drunk and talkative, interestingly so . . . Phase two: very drunk, argumentative and malicious . . . Phase three: dead drunk and incoherent. In the final phase he was like a boxer out on his feet still going through the motions of throwing punches; the words still flowed but they were meaningless. At this stage it was unfortunate that he did not have a wife to turn the tap off by bundling him into a taxi and taking him home.

Often this fell to the lot of a male friend, as was to be the case with Jack House when Gilbert was doing *Round Britain Quiz*. Another who had a session of it was Charles Hamblett. He was a staff writer with *John Bull* and when he was writing Gilbert's autobiography for him he was well equipped not only to write the story but also to cope with what was likely to arise through his liking for a drink. Was he not at that time acting as what might be termed a wet nurse for Dylan Thomas when the Welsh wild man would come up on visits to London ?

Of the two, Gilbert was probably the easier to handle since he was not the messy drunk that Dylan Thomas was. Hamblett would be the poet's drinking companion at a pub around the corner from his St John's Wood flat known as 'Rosie's' and now rebuilt as the 'Rosetti' and nick-

26

named the 'Golder's Green Annexe' through being adopted by the young Jews of that publess part of London. At Rosie's, Dylan Thomas would hold court with his shirt hanging out and waving his pint of beer, and be very entertaining indeed until closing time when it was necessary to get him, somehow, back to the flat. And not infrequently would local citizens, taking a late evening stroll around the delightful byways of St John's Wood, come across Dylan Thomas being sick out of a window of the Hambletts' ground floor flat. It was not the sort of thing associated with Gilbert Harding, but there were of course those other hazards. When Hamblett had taken him to a quiet hotel on the Isle of Wight to get the book finished they returned to the mainland with a sticking plaster plainly to be seen on Gilbert's upper lip. Harding had been involved in one of what he habitually described as 'disfiguring incidents'.

After three terms (par for the course?) at Antigonish he felt 'restless and jaded' and 'without protracted farewell on either side' he returned to England. He had managed to run through five teaching jobs in the four years since he had left Cambridge.

His next stop (brief) was Arundel, where he taught at a crammer's in the shadow of the huge Victorian mansion built to look like a Mediaeval castle and lived in the cottage where A. J. Cronin had written *The Citadel*.

He found 'cramming much better than teaching little boys in a school or adolescents in a university. At least the assumption is that one's pupils really want to learn in order to get through their exams as quickly as possible. There is a better relationship between master and pupil together when both are working for a common object rather than sparring resentfully against each other.'

The chauffeur driven car which was all part of the Gilbert Harding image when he achieved fame and the fact that he never drove himself stemmed from his period in Arundel. He bought his first and the only motor car he owned for personal motoring, in order to go for 'spins' around the delightful Sussex countryside. It was second-hand Jowett for which he paid a mere £15, which has a nostalgic ring to it, as does the fact that he could buy the car and at once set off at the wheel of it for a spin. You could do that in those days, provided you had the 5-shillings to put down for a driving licence, there being no silly nonsense then of having to go through a driving test – a contributing factor to the statistics which reveal that annual deaths on the road in the 1930s roughly parallel those of today, in spite of there having been less than a quarter of the vehicles out and about now. Harding himself almost became a statistic several times. He soon came to the conclusion that he had neither the manners nor the temper to drive a car, disposed of the Jowett and never touched a steering wheel again.

Writing in 1953 about his younger days, Harding said:

> It was while I was at Arundel in 1931 that I met Hilaire Belloc and G.K. Chesterton. It was one of those unsatisfactory meetings when there is so much you wish to say and yet nothing ever comes of it. Belloc, in any case, insisted on being very grand, remaining seated in the back of a limousine, 'receiving'.
>
> I wish I had seen more of Chesterton in that period. But I was shy of making approaches to great men, so I am grateful to record a visit to lunch at Beaconsfield. We talked happily through lunch and then, with some surprise, we suddenly discovered that it was one o'clock the next day. During those twelve hours we had effectively contradicted ourselves scores of times on the subject of God, poetry, capitalism and the Roman Catholic Church. Chesterton's delightful gift of paradox was at its best and we laughed uproariously in the balmy Buckinghamshire air as we wandered (I seem to remember) through the garden, he talking, I listening, in defence of Christian morals and of the glories of human faith. As he spoke, it seemed to me that the world became a rich and good place in which to live, and something of the magic has stayed in my bones. I now know that whatever disasters may befall me or however desperately circumstances may afflict me, I had had a brief insight into the true purpose and dignity of life. Falter and deviate as we may, there is in each of us a pinch of grace which deserves – and sometimes achieves – recognition.
>
> When at last I was preparing to take my leave from this hospitable man, I remember saying: 'I'm afraid I talked an awful lot.'
>
> 'Oh, no,' replied Chesterton, 'you are a wonderful conversationalist. You let me do all the talking, which is as it should be, young Gilbert.'

His stay at the crammer's at Arundel was made a brief one by the arrival of a letter from the Cambridge Appointments Board recommending him to the post of English teacher in the Franco-Britannique school at the University of Clermont Ferrand, near Vichy in the Auvergne. His sojourn there was even shorter than the three terms which seemed customary for him. It occupied merely the three summer months of 1932 and then he was back in England teaching at a Catholic private school, where he quickly came to dislike the headmaster as much as the headmaster disliked him.

He did not exactly leave; he was precipitated from the school following an outspoken comment of the type that some twenty years later was to get him into trouble on television.

One of the boys was son of a General whose family had been in the army as far back as the records go. The lad was naturally earmarked for the soldiery but one day he confided in Harding: his was a horsey family but he did not merely want to ride horses, he wanted to be a veterinary surgeon. Later when Harding heard that the boy had failed his entrance to Woolwich, he wrote him: 'I am sorry you failed, but you will be much better employed curing sick horses than killing healthy men.'

Unfortunately the General found the letter and a few days afterwards Harding was summoned by the headmaster.

'Am I to understand you are preaching seditious nonsense to the boys?' he fumed.

Harding asked him what he meant and the headmaster read from a letter he had received from the General, couched in violent terms and ending with the recommendation that he should be horsewhipped. 'And so you should,' the headmaster added.

The boy did pass his entrance exam for military school at the second attempt and emerged as a regular army officer just in time to be one of the first to be killed in action in World War II.

Harding's connection with the Catholic prep. school severed, he headed for Bradford for Christmas ('depressed and – as usual – penniless') and was back living with his mother at the Bowling Park institution for the poor, where she was now the Matron.

CHAPTER 5

POLICE CONSTABLE HARDING

Anyone remembering Gilbert Harding at the height of his television fame would find it hard to credit that he had been a policeman on the beat. Admittedly it had been twenty years previously, in 1932 when the 25-year-old Gilbert had returned to live with his mother in Bradford after his unsatisfactory time as teacher at the Catholic private school. Jobless again, he paid 25s. a week to stay with her at the Bowling Park Poor Law Institution and for something to do he used to drop in at the police courts and the quarter sessions. 'The law has always fascinated me,' he often said. It was linked with his interest in religion. 'After all,' he would say, 'weren't the first lawmakers the priests ?'

At the courts he used to chat with the constables and officials and when he met Deputy Chief Constable Petty it was suggested that Gilbert join the force. He was soon made aware, however, that coming in at that gentleman's instigation brought no privileges; it was no quick answer to dreams of a Scotland Yard posting. He was kitted out in the uniform which he found 'cuts you off from your fellow men', had to don 'that terrible headgear' and was launched on his thirteen weeks' training.

For the gregarious Gilbert the immediate outcome of being in a policeman's uniform was probably the unhappiest aspect of his new job. In a tram on his way to the gym for P.T. training, for example, he would start to strike up a conversation with someone, only to find that they edged away from him. He was at once made conscious of what he felt was the lasting psychological effect of threats in childhood of 'the policeman will get you if you don't behave yourself'.

The work-outs in the gym were also among the jobs less pleasing aspects to one who had never shone at sport or other physical activity. But he stuck it through, not without coming a particularly bad cropper when he misjudged a manoeuvre on the vaulting horse and sustained a knee injury which not only resulted in his graduating from trainee to constable on the beat with a limp but which plagued him for the rest of his life.

Gilbert was not sure whether it was because in his Division there was a lack of confidence in his capabilities as a copper but he did feel that he was more often than was usual assigned to the lack-lustre shift of 10 p.m. to 6 a.m. About all a policeman is called upon to do in that period, once the pub-emptying has been dealt with, is to patrol the deserted streets 'trying out', which is the police term for checking that the front doors of buildings and shops are locked. Rarely was there any action, especially in the 1930's in Bradford, a town which could scarcely had been said to have been lively even in the daylight hours.

He recalled one night, however, when a carload of revellers were in an 'open tourer' of the type popular in those days weaving its way along an empty street. He stepped out to halt them and when the car stopped he had some difficulty in asserting his authority. The reason for this was that one of the girls said: 'Where's the fancy dress ball? You're no copper. You're having us on.' Deeply hurt, Harding did his utmost to convince them he was genuine but they would have none of it. At length one youth leaned out of the open car and tried to pull off Harding's 'false' moustache. Humiliated, Gilbert announced that they had just five seconds to get themselves on their way.

Gilbert's career as a policeman was, however, marked by one incident which was far from humdrum. On the beat one day he came to a tram that had been halted and in which there seemed to be some sort of commotion. He got on board and found that a pregnant woman had mistimed the coming event and was in labour. The motorman and the conductor were arranging for her to be assisted from the tram. There was no verbatim report of what ensued but the gist of it was:

Harding: 'Do not touch that good woman. She must not be moved.'

'But –' from the motorman.

'Keeping to your petty little time-tables is of complete unimportance at the moment. You would risk the well-being of this lady and the life of her child-to-be by manhandling her out into the street! Summon a doctor. Anyone here know about midwifery? Someone go to the nearest chemist's and get whatever is appropriate to the occasion . . .'

Gilbert, as assertive now as he had not been with the revellers because he felt this was a matter of life and death, was adamant. The woman was advanced in labour. She must have the baby where she was.

Anybody who lived through the era of the tramcar, now generally a thing of the past, knows that when a tram is stuck on the line others pile up behind it, a bottleneck develops, motor traffic in both ways is blocked. Just such a situation built up as the result of P.C. Harding's decision and as the accouchement took its course Bradford was to have the most mammoth traffic jam ever experienced there, before or since.

But that was an isolated imprint Harding the policeman left on

Bradford. He returned to the trudge of life on the beat, until it came home to him that this was not really his true way of life.

He was coming off duty one evening and, standing there in uniform at the doorway of the police station, he hesitated as he realised it was teeming with rain. Two new young constables on the night shift started laughing at him and one of them called out: 'What's the matter, professor? Have you forgotten your umbrella?'

Relating this to a friend later, he said: 'I didn't resent their attitude. They were right. They were young men fitting securely into their niche of being policemen. I was a pudgy, limping oddity. I was a misfit there. Having thought it over when I was walking home through the rain, I announced to my mother: " I'm never going to walk the beat again." '

By happy coincidence his mother had been waiting for him with some good news. Someone had been trying to get in touch with him from London with the offer of a teaching job. It turned out to be the Director of Education of Cyprus, who had come over to arrange the appointment of an English master for a school in Limassol. Harding, during his out of work period, had sent off applications far and wide for teaching jobs and one of them had come home to roost.

CHAPTER 6

JOURNALIST? BARRISTER?
BROADCASTER?

When Harding reported for duty at the Limassol Greek Gymnasium in Cyprus he found the same sort of problem in teaching the boys English as he encountered with the French-Canadian students in Nova Scotia – a dislike of England and therefore her language.

He had arrived in Cyprus at an unfortunate time. It was shortly after the rebellion of 1931 when the Enosis movement for union with Greece, led by the bishops, had burnt down Government buildings. The Legislative Assembly had been abolished and the Governor ruled the island by decree. Under the influence of Enosis, the boys were unresponsive and recalcitrant towards their English master. Inside the classroom Gilbert did what he could and outside it he enjoyed the sun-drenched life which could not have been further removed from the grey life in Bradford.

With brandy at two shillings a bottle and wine less expensive, that aspect which loomed so large throughout his adult life was well looked after. He explored the historic sites of Cyprus. Instead of staying at the fashionable Continental Hotel, where those of the English colony who were married lived, he chose a small good hotel in one of the back streets so that he could be among the locals as he set about learning modern Greek. Helped by his photographic memory he was not long in conquering the language and also in acquiring Turkish during sojourns in the Turkish part of the island. His adding these two languages to the French and German he already had was to prove a prime reason why he was sought out by the BBC and launched on his career as a broadcaster.

When from time to time he was invited to dinner at Government House he could observe with amused detachment the protocol which he felt must surely have been more strictly adhered to than at Buckingham Palace. He could afford to be detached about 'the ludicrously formal and pompous proceedings' since, as a mere teacher and not a colonial administrator, protocol placed him at the bottom of every list. He enjoyed the embarrassment of Admiral Sir Roger Backhouse, who dropped in at the island in *Revenge* to show the flag and gave a party on board for a select few of the local dignitaries and Harding was invited by mistake. 'Oh, well,' he said as he surveyed the school teacher in tails borrowed from a man of considerably different build, 'since you are here I suppose the only thing we can do is make the best of it.'

At the English Club, where the atmosphere was pure Somerset Maugham, he more than once found himself in trouble through his talent, highly developed later in life, for saying the wrong thing, or the right thing when it would have been better left unsaid. Once when members were criticising Mussolini for locking up people without trial and he commented that such criticism seemed odd since the same sort of thing was going on in Cyprus, the doyen of the club, Colonel Gallagher, ex-Chief of Police, pointed to the door and thundered: 'Get out of the club, sir. We want none of your nasty, snivelling long-haired Cambridge-Communist nonsense here.'

He was re-instated but incurred Colonel Gallagher's wrath again when he remarked to him: 'You know why the sun never sets on the British Empire, don't you? It doesn't trust it.'

Twenty years later such comments were to create a public outcry when Gilbert, during a *What's My Line?* broadcast, referred to 'the chinless idiots who made that evil thing, the British Empire.' The indignation which that caused was to receive wide press coverage.

The interesting thing about the public image projected by Gilbert Harding the famous broadcaster – the insults, the outrageous behaviour, the unexpected kindness – was that it was not something specially evolved and exaggerated as part of his professional make-up, like Magnus Pyke's panic handwaving. Gilbert had always been like that; it was merely that on radio and TV it was before a much larger audience.

Christopher Sykes recalls his arrival by ship at Cyprus with Gilbert, and as they were going ashore by tender the 28 year-old Gilbert created a scene about his luggage being mislaid. A tall, weak, moustached young man who looked somewhat ridiculous in a Homburg hat too big for him said to Gilbert: 'You don't seem to be in the best of tempers today, old man.' Gilbert turned on him. 'No, I am not, and it doesn't put me in a better one to see you grinning at me with that inane bloody face of yours either!' Ashamed of his outburst afterwards, Gilbert was embarrassed to find that the young man was the clerk in his bank who usually chased his cheques and he met him often outside the bank. 'But he had his uses,' Gilbert told Sykes years later. 'He was an antidote to my rudeness. I just had to keep my tongue in check whenever he was around.'

Similarly in Cyprus the young Harding displayed the other side to his nature which was to endear him to so many people in his mature years – his kindness and understanding. An amiable spinster was in good standing in the English community with her amusing stories about a famous North of England poet and novelist whom she said was a very good friend of hers. News came that he was to visit Cyprus and Gilbert was given the job of organising a reception for him. He hurried around to the poet's friend, knowing how thrilled she would be to hear about it. But she was not pleased. She broke down and confessed that it was all a lie. She had never met the man. She was going to be humiliated. 'Leave it to me,' said Gilbert. 'Come to the reception. I'll arrange something with your – er – friend.' What he did was have a quiet chat with the poet before the reception and when the woman arrived the eminent visitor welcomed her happily, chided her for not letting him know she was in Cyprus and launched into recollections of all the occasions they had enjoyed together. 'It was one of the most wonderful things that has ever happened to me,' she said with tears of gratitude to Gilbert afterwards.

Such acts of kindness interspersed with his rudeness, to the extent of its being branded 'outrageous behaviour', were to cause those who believe in horoscopes to point to Harding as living proof of the authenticity of the signs of the zodiac. Was he not the epitome of a Gemini – the Twins, a split personality?

Throughout his public life the adjective most used in his regard was *irascible*. Madeline Scott, wife of the man in whose arms he died, described his outbreaks of temper as 'like somebody accidentally letting off a pistol in the living room', as the unfortunate Cyprus bank clerk could have confirmed. But on the other side of the coin ... James Barrie once said, 'The very best sort of kindness is kindness by stealth.' Typical of Gilbert in later years was what happened when a friend looked rather harassed and he asked him what was the trouble. 'Nothing really', was the reply. 'It's just that we're getting our son off to boarding school.' Gilbert asked the name of the school. When the boy arrived there he found on his bed in the dormitory an envelope containing a £5 note. There was nothing to say who it had come from.

Arthur Godfrey, who is with the *Richmond and Twickenham Times*, ran a thriving mixed youth club in that district where Gilbert was living when he began to achieve fame. 'His reputation, as you know, was of a rather ferocious, ill-tempered man,' he said to me. 'But he accepted an invitation to spend an evening talking to the teenage club members and was kind, wise and sympathetic and he created a most favourable impression. Unlike some other prominent TV and radio people living in the Richmond area, Gilbert Harding did not seek publicity locally and whatever he did to help a good cause was done quietly and out of the goodness of his heart'.

At the height of his fame he constantly received letters asking for help and countless times he responded, with things like toys for deprived youngsters or paying for someone to have a holiday; but when it required quite an outlay, as with the latter, his secretary Roger Storey said that he would not do so until he had made enquiries – 'He did not want to be taken for a sucker.'

The explosive side of his character would mean that often he could be rude to a friend or someone else closely associated with him in his radio and TV work. The explosion would be followed by abject apologies. 'Contrition was a great thing with Gilbert,' said Alan Melville. His mother once snapped at him: 'One of these days, Gilbert, you are going to do your apologising act and find that it's too late.'

Anona Winn found that his habit of sending flowers by way of apology extended to her family. After one of the numerous rows between them, Gilbert learned that her mother was ill in a nursing home in Haslemere and the place was showered by what Anona called 'Constance Spry creations'. Her mother had her moment of reflected glory when the nurses were able to floralise all the rooms of the neighbouring patients as well as Mrs Winn's room, and the staff and walking wounded crowded around her bed saying 'You know Gilbert Harding?'

His florists in Brighton could be said to have been among the chief mourners at his death. Never before or since have they had such a good customer.

But to return to the young, in no way famous Harding in Cyprus . . . Low as he was in the pecking order in the English community there, being only a teacher, his status received a boost when he was able to announce that *The Times* had appointed him 'Our Correspondent' in Cyprus. (In point of fact he was just a 'stringer' – a person on the spot available to file the occasional story – but who was to know the difference?) He was to say at that time that he was toying with the idea of becoming a journalist and indeed when he left Cyprus to return to England it was with the intention of trying his luck in Fleet Street.

However, his first sally into the field of journalism did not seem to have been very successful. If *The Times* had expected some revealing despatches from that politically disturbed island, they do not appear to have received them. Looking back years later on his period as a *Times* correspondent, the only story he could remember doing was an interview with Jean Batten. This New Zealand pilot ranked with Amelia Earheart and Amy Mollison in those pre-Women's Lib days when women held their own with men pioneering the world's air routes, and she had touched down at a landing strip in Cyprus to refuel before continuing her solo flight from Australia to England. As soon as the interview was over she was up and away again and Gilbert went back to his digs, to try laboriously to get it down on paper. The written word did not then or ever come easily to him; Harding reflected: 'I cannot remember what the flier said or what I wrote, but I rather feel that she reached London before my report reached Printing House Square.'

The upheaval of people's lives by the world war which was shortly to break out did have its compensations for many, and Gilbert Harding was among them. It is interesting to conjecture what course his life would have taken had not the advent of war brought him into the BBC, for him to discover ultimately what he really *was* good at. Without that catalyst, would he have continued to drift aimlessly from job to job, to wind up the born loser he showed every indication of being? And by the same token would *What's My Line?*, the keystone of his fame, have been the same compulsive viewing without him? Eamonn Andrews, Isobel Barnett, Barbara Kelly, Jerry Desmonde and David Nixon were television performers of little experience at the outset. As a Hardingless team, would they have been the stuff of which programmes that become a national obsession are made?

On his return from Cyprus he had at least made an attempt to be more incisive about his rôle in life and to offset the fact that since leaving Cambridge his 'career' had very much fallen in line with Bernard Shaw's maxim – 'Those who can, do, and those who can't, teach.' To further his decision that journalism was his true niche in life he went hopefully to Printing House Square, only to learn that *The Times* – who could blame them? – hardly thought their former Cyprus correspondent should be taken on staff.

Recovering from that setback, he decided that Law would be the thing for him. From a friend he had made in Cyprus he got a letter of introduction which enabled him to become a member of the Honourable Society of Gray's Inn and began to 'eat his dinners', which it may come as a surprise to some to learn, means study for the Bar.

To finance his studies he took a job at Marcy's, the crammers', in Chancery Lane and embarked on what for him was a happy period of helping young men to get into university on one side of the street and crossing over to the other side to attend his law lectures.

'He would have made an extremely good barrister,' John Freeman once said of him, and undoubtedly Gilbert Harding in action in the law courts – particularly as an advocate – could have produced some memorable moments.

However, the war intervened before he could take his final exams and it was to the BBC he was called, not the Bar, and he was started on his route towards becoming the nation's most talked-about broad-caster. It was not through any decision of his own. He had never had any ambitions in the direction of radio or television. Somebody else made the decision for him.

When the war was in its early, so-called phoney stage and His Majesty's Services were not yet ready for Gilbert Harding, he received from out of the blue a telegram from the BBC asking him if he would be interested in joining their Overseas Service. The fact that he was known by a former Cambridge colleague, Kenneth Adam, at the BBC to have French, German and (from his time in Cyprus) modern Greek and Turkish was instrumental in his being considered for that branch of the corporation.

The section of the BBC's overseas operation to which Gilbert was assigned was the Monitoring Service and he was installed in an office on the second floor of Broadcasting House in what to him seemed a curious job. 'The BBC had set up a listening service in the country (at Evesham, but that was very hush-hush) where, in considerable discomfort and under cloak-and-dagger supervision, people of all nationalities listened to foreign broadcasts in practically every language. These would be translated into English and sent by teleprinter to London, where people like me would be employed as sub-editors to make a "daily digest of foreign broadcasts".

'Most of my colleagues had been recruited from Fleet Street but for some reason I was singled out to be chief sub-editor and then was elevated to an "Information Bureau Supervisor", with scrambled messages coming in on the teleprinters, "hot lines" to the Service Chiefs so that "flashes" could be relayed to them of anything immediate, and all in all a glorious kind of Phillips Oppenheim atmosphere.'

The whole of the BBC's Monitoring Service had been in London at the beginning of the war but when the bombing started the 'listeners' were evacuated to the secret location in the Cotswolds, to a stately home two miles outside Evesham.

'Wood Norton' had been built in the last century by the exiled Duc d'Orleans and later occupied by the King of Portugal in exile. When the BBC took over Wood Norton there was a relatively small staff, housed in the main building of the estate, but as the Czech-born Ewald Osers recounted: 'As the Germans overran each new country, people who knew that language had to be added to the staff. Nissen huts sprouted up in the grounds. It soon began to look like some sort of base camp. What had once been beautiful lawns became a sea of mud. Except in the height of summer we had to wear gumboots all the time and were huddled up in all the woollens we could lay hands on. It was a weird sort of scene, the contrast of the academics who did the actual listening to the broadcasts and analysing them, and the radio technicians, teleprinter operators, canteen workers and all the other people needed to maintain a round-the-clock service, all mucking in together. By the time Hitler launched his attack on Russia and a Russian contingent was added to the personnel, there were more than a thousand working there. Of course there wasn't room enough to live as well as work there. We were billeted out on the local populace.'

Gilbert Harding was transferred to Evesham and he stood out as someone always to be remembered by Osers. 'I shall never forget his unfailing kindness to us refugees. He was genuinely interested in what we and our families had gone through before we were able to get out and over to Britain. And what I particularly liked about him was this. We were the butt of a lot of jokes, especially in regard to our "fractured English", as you might call it. For instance, I remember one of us in a pub one night, I think he was a Pole. Anyway, he felt he was making good progress with colloquial English, everyday words and expressions. He had learned that a publican was called "the guv'nor" and this night when we went into the pub the landlord's wife didn't seem to be around. So this chap said to him, "Where's the governess tonight?" He never heard the last of that. We were always made fun of, but Gilbert never laughed at our mistakes. He used to take us aside quietly and explain and correct them.'

Again the kindness of Gilbert Harding ... Similar to what had happened at Evesham was another example when he had come up in the world and was a member of the Savage Club.

There was a member who was a front-runner among the club's bores. A guest taken to the club by Harding met him and said to Gilbert afterwards, 'He seems rather a boring person.' 'Boring!' said Gilbert. 'Dear boy, he bores for England.' One evening at the bar the gentleman concerned, having bored everyone to distraction, made to go but said, 'I think I'll have just one more for the road.' More than once. When it happened next time, Gilbert turned to him and said, 'Don't change the subject. You were saying goodbye.' The man, incensed by the good reception this got from members within earshot, happened to have influence with the committee and on the basis of this and other comments Harding had directed towards him it was decided that he should be barred. When the waiters and others on the staff learned of this they sent a deputation to the committee to point out that Mr Harding was always most thoughtful towards them – and took a great and genuine interest in them, their families and their problems. It wound up with an ultimatum – 'If Mr Harding goes, we go.' Mr Harding stayed.

In 1944 the BBC decided to transfer Harding to Toronto, to be liaison man with the Canadian Broadcasting Corporation, but he did not leave Evesham before 'the night Gilbert chopped down the grand piano' had become a legend at the Monitoring Service.

It happened on the evening the main building caught fire. Although enemy bombers were in action that night they had not been the cause. It was an electrical fault that had set the top floor ablaze and before the Evesham fire engines could get out to the scene it was burning fiercely. The Monitoring Service was known to be on the Germans' list as a target and at the local defence headquarters they were so worried that bombers would be attracted to the fire that the R.A.F. put up fighter planes to patrol the area.

Those working in the building had been evacuated and the others came from their nearby billets to stand in the grounds and watch the blaze. Volunteers were called to go into the ground floor to salvage what they could – teleprinters, filing cabinets, typewriters – before the fire penetrated below.

Gilbert grabbed a fireman's axe and rushed in. Soon someone passing the doorway of the big recreation room was surprised to see him going to work with the axe on the grand piano which had been part of the original furnishings of the stately home. Either he was more drunk than usual or he was having a brainstorm.

'What on earth are you doing, Gilbert!' shouted someone else who came up to the doorway.

'It's a superb instrument,' he shouted back, not interrupting his blows on the piano. 'It must be saved.'

'By wrecking it with an axe?'

'Only the legs, for heaven's sake. You can't get it through the door with the legs still on.'

CHAPTER 7

TWENTY QUESTIONS

The radio quiz which was to prove the most popular ever broadcast in Britain – *Twenty Questions* – was an American import. Not that the game itself of trying to guess some object in up to twenty questions had been invented on American radio, since it was as old as *I Spy* as a way of keeping children and others amused on long train journeys and car trips. What they had done in the States was adapt it to a formalised radio programme – with Question Master, Panel and Mystery Voice – and it was the British rights to this which the BBC bought and launched in 1947.

To give it what they felt would be an appropriate trans-Atlantic flavour the BBC had a Canadian, Stewart MacPherson, as the Question Master. He had earned a certain reputation as a boxing commentator whose quick-fire, North American delivery was in sharp contrast to the coverage of Raymond Glendenning and Barrington Dalby. 'He throws a right to the head! Another right to the head! Wham! A left to the body! That one went in right up to his elbow! . . .'

When MacPherson went back to Canada, Kenneth Horne took over as Question Master and the programme jogged along with a fair amount of success until 1950, when a new man took the chair and it really came alive. What happened was that Kenneth Horne went off on an extended holiday and the BBC had to decide who was to take his place.

Harding, writing at the time when *Twenty Questions* was at the height of its success (with him as Question Master) said that he had very much hoped to get the chair when MacPherson vacated it and was thrilled at the chance of occupying it when Kenneth Horne went away.

That was not quite the truth but at that time he could hardly say otherwise, not in front of all his newly acquired fans. The recollection of Robin Russell, who shared a room with Gilbert at the BBC, is that he was hauled reluctantly from one of the BBC pubs to do the show. He did not want to do it. He felt it was beneath him.

His previous broadcasting he felt had been on a certain intellectual level. *Twenty Questions*! A mindless parlour game. He would be demeaning himself by appearing on such a programme . . .

Apart from some interviewing of servicemen during the war, his first major broadcasting for the BBC had begun in 1948. He had returned from Canada very depressed. He had passed his fortieth birthday, with what sort of future ahead? It irked him that while he had been in the Canadian wilderness, former pals of his at the BBC had now become famous broadcasters – men such as Richard Dimbleby, Wynford Vaughan-Thomas and Raymond Glendenning. The opportunity came when the BBC, having fired him and told him to freelance, put *Round Britain Quiz* his way.

Round Britain Quiz was an outgrowth of *Trans-Atlantic Quiz*, a wartime show which had had the twin purpose of providing entertainment and helping to cement Anglo-American relations. It was continued after the war but by 1948 the BBC was hit by the acute dollar shortage which affected everybody in Britain and they no longer had the appropriate finances for such a link-up. So instead they evolved a similar programme in which a London panel took on Scotland, the Midlands and other home regions. Lionel Hale, of the trans-Atlantic show, was the question master in London and Harding was given his first major assignment as a broadcaster in the same role in Scotland. He grasped the opportunity with both hands and made this the programme which newspapers in future were to label as the one in which 'he first came to public notice'.

The Scottish part of the hook-up was done in Glasgow and the panellists there were James Fergusson, later Sir James Fergusson, Bart., of Eton and Balliol, leader writer of the *Glasgow Herald*, and Jack House, a columnist with the *Glasgow Evening Citizen*.

In view of Sir James's background and the fact that one of the London panellists was Professor Denis Brogan of Cambridge, the level of the programme was on a somewhat higher plane than is usual with radio quizzes. Jack House – now 70, the precise age Harding would have been had he lived – makes no mystery of his having left school when he was 15 and he will tell you that the idea was that he and Sir James should complement one another. When Gilbert had first met James Fergusson and Jack House in connection with the show, he wondered how listeners would be able to distinguish between what were to him similar Scottish accents.

'I don't think they'll find any great difficulty,' House said. 'James speaks with a public school accent, while mine is a public house one.'

Question Master Harding and Sir James could also be said to be very different and although it did not make itself evident on the air, off the air they most certainly did not dovetail. Sir James, who was to aspire to the venerated Scottish post of Keeper of the Records, tended towards the strait-laced approach to life. Gilbert Harding's way of life was the direct antithesis of this, for if ever a man could be seen to be drinking it was Gilbert. So when the morning's work at the studio was finished and Gilbert set off to unwind, Sir James preferred not to be around. It always fell to the lot of Jack House to do the entertaining of their co-broadcaster up from London. However, as far as 'entertaining Gilbert' was concerned House soon ran into a major problem. Harding always insisted on gourmet food and drink and a time came when House was running out of good restaurants he could take him back to.

There had been the incident at the highly rated Glaswegian eating place, Mal Maison, which had revolved around Gilbert falling sound asleep in the middle of the meal. Deciding to take him instead to The Bank restaurant, House warned him it was in the middle of Glasgow's rag trade district and therefore much frequented by Jews. Looking hurt at what House had implied, Gilbert said: 'Do you think I'm intolerant?' During drinks at the bar he so incensed a 'wee Jew' that the small gentleman invited him outside where, as House retailed it, 'he clocked him.' 'Another restaurant off the list,' House said to himself, but eventually he found a haven in the Queen Anne, a then well known Glasgow restaurant since burnt down. It was run by the Bells, father and son, and they were so taken with Gilbert Harding as a radio performer that they were prepared to be accommodating.

When *Round Britain Quiz* was switched to an afternoon broadcast from Edinburgh, Gilbert went alone to the Queen Anne for a farewell lunch with the Bells because they had been so good to him. Before the meal they asked him what he would like to drink and when he said gin-and-French a bottle of gin and a bottle of Noilly-Prat were set up on the table before him. Having made inroads into that, Harding was provided with two bottles of champagne during the meal. At the end a bottle of their best brandy was opened for him. When Jack House met him at Glasgow's Central Station to take the train to Edinburgh he was, 'very much in a state of disrepair'.

That train trip is a mere forty-five minutes but long enough to have a leisurely afternoon tea so House, mindful of its sobering influence, took Harding straight to the restaurant car. However, the train had barely moved off when Gilbert reached into his overnight bag and brought forth what was left of the bottle of brandy. The waiters were just half way through their ritual of toasted tea cakes, bread and jam, cakes and 'More tea?' when Gilbert was seen, and heard, to be fast asleep. As the train drew in to Edinburgh's old Prince's Street station, House woke him up and said, 'We're here.' Gilbert looked at him. 'Good heavens,' he said. 'London already?'

Booking into the Caledonian Hotel, Harding saw to it that his regular bottle of whisky was there available for him in his room as he got ready

43

to go to the studio. When the quiz team assembled there and the hook-up with London was established, House was yet again amazed that Harding's performance gave no hint whatsoever of what had gone before.

Jack House regarded him as a 'really outstanding chairman'. He felt it was invidious to name those who took over Harding's job in *Round Britain Quiz* when he was no longer free to do it but none of them, in his view, was capable of handling it the way he did. The programme was 'never the same', despite the fact that *they* were invariably approaching each broadcast cold sober.

When the BBC decided to revive the wartime *Brains Trust*, the success of Harding on *Round Britain Quiz* prompted them to put him in the chair. He felt he was in his element among the intellectuals. Here was the boy from the workhouse rubbing shoulders with Lord Samuel, Bertrand Russell, Kingsley Martin, Lady Bonham-Carter, Dr Bronowski, Julian Huxley. He had come a long way! He felt that intellectually he could hold his own in their company. But one could detect that he was always deferential towards people such as they. The snobbish side of his character kept him in awe of them. The rudeness for which he was to become renowned (THE MAN WHO WON FAME FOR RUDE-NESS was his obituary headline in the *Daily Herald*) was never directed towards them or others of their ilk he encountered in his day to day life. It was reserved for people whom he did not respect.

As well as those already mentioned there were two other *Brains Trust* regulars. Commander A.B. Campbell, R.N. (Ret.), could be relied upon to add a dash of salty humour to his philosophising and he had a fund of tall stories, practically all of which started with 'When I was in Patagonia . . . .' Professor C.E.M. Joad had a catchphrase as familiar as any from the current comedy shows. Joad's brilliantly analytical mind required him to get his terms of reference straight before embarking on an intellectual balloon ascension and he was so often heard to intone 'It all depends what you mean by . . .' The wags of the saloon bar soon took this up and were saying 'It all depends what you mean by' anything from 'a pint of bitter' to 'the Cheltenham Gold Cup'.

Joad's bearded, perky face became well known through publicity surrounding his appearance on the *Brains Trust* but a certain ticket collector on a train in which he was travelling either never read the papers or was unimpressed by the Professor's reputation. In those days even though there were only two classes on trains, as now, they were called First and Third, and Joad was found to be sitting in luxury in a First Class compartment with a Third Class ticket. After he had been fined for the offence he happened to be on a radio programme with

Randolph Churchill (known to his host of non-admirers as 'Also Randolph') and the two had a heated argument on the air about something or other, Randolph getting in the last word by accusing Joad of being 'a third class Socrates'.

It was Charmian Innes, an ebullient young entertainer who was to be-become quite well known in the 1950s, who first suggested to BBC producer Pat Dixon shortly after the war that a battle of the sexes on the air would make for lively listening and *We Beg To Differ* had become a successful programme. Roy Plomley was the chairman as a male and a female panel aired their views on such varied topics as child-rearing and why women squeeze the toothpaste tube in the middle. A regular panellist was Dr Charles Hill, who had earned his fame as the Radio Doctor and had become the darling of the hypochondriacs through his total lack of self-consciousness in discussing on the air such things as bowel movements.

When Dr (eventually Lord) Hill had to stop broadcasting on becoming a Parliamentary candidate in 1949 Gilbert was brought in, and it was on this programme that he sowed the seeds of what was to be projected as 'the Harding image'.

On *Round Britain Quiz* and the *Brains Trust* he had been – when broadcasting, at least – on his best behaviour in the semi-intellectual atmosphere of serious discussion with university dons and the like. The snob in him would not permit his kicking over the traces in such company. But now, on *We Beg To Differ*, it was more of a showbiz climate. Besides Chairman Innes, regulars on the women's side of the fence were Joyce Grenfell and Gladys Young, and two of the leading opponents were the happily married couple Kay Hammond and John Clements who, according to Gilbert, 'would counter each other's views with some stingingly effective retort and then exchange quick private smiles', unseen by the listening millions.

Among such people he could be more natural. He soon earned 'public notoriety as a cantankerous, opinionated bachelor' and an abrupt comment he made to Dr Edith Summerskill was the starting point of his reputation for bluntness, the beginning of his reputation as 'Mr Rude of broadcasting'.

However, this was just the prelude to the show which was to make him a nationally known personality.

His initial reluctance to appear on *Twenty Questions* had stemmed from the fact that his first major programme, *Round Britain Quiz*, if not intellectual had at least been on a higher plane than the average quiz; on the *Brains Trust* he had definitely been up among the intellectuals;

45

on *We Beg To Differ* he could give free rein to his intellect by indulging in one of his favourite pastimes – expounding. But *Twenty Questions* would really be lowering his sights.

It is interesting that just as he had got into broadcasting in the first place not by any choice of his own, not because he felt that that was where his talents lay, in the same way he was forced into participation in a radio 'parlour game'. His future was worked out for him by other people. It was not he who decided that Question Master of *Twenty Questions* was the sort of thing he could do well, as indeed proved to be the case. And from this start, it was decided – by other people – that he would be just the person to do well on another parlour game, this time on television. His fame stemmed entirely from his appearances on *Twenty Questions* and *What's My Line?* and this was the root cause of his discontent. John Freeman said: 'He had the brains and imagination to do some great work in life.' Harding felt his was a wasted intellect.

He always felt self-conscious about 'getting so much for doing so little'. The money-for-jam aspect of being a quiz performer is well known to all of us who have augmented our bank accounts in this easy way. There are no rehearsals, no script to learn. You just *appear*. On the evening of the broadcast you merely arrive at the studio in sufficient time for the producer not to be worried about you not turning up. You and the other participants then hang around in the wings while the producer gives the audience a warm-up talk, after which each in turn is introduced to the applauding audience. You take your place at the long table for the panellists or the desk for the Question Master and time-keeper opposite, and the producer goes off to the control room. The second hand creeps around to broadcast time, throats are cleared and sips of water taken. The red light goes on. Your are on the air. For the next half hour you make whatever contributions to the proceedings come to mind and try to be as bright as possible. The programme ends. Some people rush up from the audience for autographs. Then with the others on the show and various hangers-on you go to a local pub to have a post mortem on the evenings' activities and get in some solid drinking, which is known in the trade as 'unwinding'. Then home, safe in the knowledge that there will be a nice cheque in the post for you in a couple of days' time, this welcome money coming along each week for the run of your contract. Never has the cliché 'it beats working for a living' been more true.

What makes it even more attractive is that invariably there are repeat fees to be picked up. As far as *Twenty Questions* was concerned, in addition to the actual live broadcast there were *seven* repeats each week – two at home and five transmissions of the recording overseas. So it added up to a very worthwhile weekly payment.

The cast of *Twenty Questions* used to worry about Gilbert's drinking. On the face of it, this seemed a thoughtful thing to do. They seemed to be genuinely concerned about him and the harm his drinking was doing to his general well-being. But a cynic would observe that, since Gilbert Harding was the key man on the programme, if he were to arrive at the studio 'drunk and incapable' (of appearing on the show), it would mean cancellation of the broadcast and no easy money in the post that week. So – 'Has Gilbert arrived . . . is he – er – all right ?' was the pre-broadcast chorus.

Harding never did cause the live transmission to be cancelled through inability to perform because of drink but, as we shall see in a moment, there was a famous occasion which came to be known as 'the night Gilbert was drunk on *Twenty Questions*'. Norman Hackforth, the Mystery Voice, whose contribution to the show was to say 'The next object is Such-and -Such' at various times, was very annoyed after that contretemps.

He wrote of the incident: 'The powers-that-be at the BBC were furious and rightly decided that the recording was too bad to be repeated. So they cancelled the repeats for that week and we all lost our repeat fees. Gilbert did write to us an abject letter of apology but we were all pretty cross at this terrible debacle and it took a lot of forgiving.'

The unpredictable Harding behaviour on the programme was half the fun of listening to *Twenty Questions* and more than once he had to be rested from it following a spot of bother of his making. One such was in 1951 when, not realising that the mike was live, he was so irked by the introductions of the panellists to the studio audience that he fumed: 'This is the last time we have any of this nonsense . . . now let's see what we can make of this show after this horrid and unsettling start.' Headlines about HARDING IN TROUBLE AGAIN in the next day's papers . . . taken off the air and replaced for the next edition of the programme by John Arlott.

John Arlott was then and still is, more than a quarter of a century later, in a class by himself as a cricket commentator. Also, then and still today, he is no mean connoisseur of wine. But master as he was of calling the shots at cricket and knowing his vintages he was not a patch on Harding when it came to conducting a *Twenty Questions* session. Nobody could do it quite like Harding and after Arlott's spell from the nursery end, the programme's seven million fans happily greeted Gilbert's return.

But Gilbert's temporary absences from the programme because the BBC felt he was in need of a rest were nothing compared to the big blow-up of 1952. Writing of the affair some time later, Harding said: 'I was perfectly sober that night, but had had a frustrating, wearing day during which everything seemed to have gone wrong. I arrived at the studio late, a thing which rarely happens . . .'

This was partially accurate. It was indeed true that he was rarely late, but as regards being 'perfectly sober' . . . he gave the impression of being very drunk indeed. For once his ability to consume great quantities of liquor before a broadcast and not show it on the air let him down.

Having taken his chair just thirty seconds before they were due to start, 'one of those dreadful things that used to happen in films to W.C. Fields happened to me. I got into a terrible muddle with the headphones. The cord got tangled and, seeing the red light flicker to show that we were on the air, I tugged at it in a sort of split-second panic and dropped the headphones.' The continuity announcer had introduced the programme to the listening millions and when all they got was the bang and clatter of the Harding headphones, he said: 'They do not seem to be ready for us in the *Twenty Questions* studio.' After this understatement the programme was cut off the air and the announcer did some waffle while Gilbert got himself and the headphones organised.

'A minute later the headphones were untangled and the programme began, but the accumulation of the day's petty irritations ending with this entanglement had aggravated my temper to the point of no return.'

When Jack Train guessed one of the objects quickly, shouting 'A Peony . . . A Peony!', and Harding failed to hear him, Train protested indignantly when the panel exhausted their twenty questions and that indeed proved to be the answer. Harding silenced him with a brusque 'Let's move on' and in that sort of confusion and back chat between question master and panel the programme stuttered to its conclusion, when Gilbert thoroughly put the lid on things by not, as was usual, announcing the result but instead saying: 'I suppose I ought to let you know the score. If you've been listening you won't need it, and if you haven't you won't want it anyway!'

That concluded the broadcast portion of the proceedings. Off the air, an almighty row developed in the studio sparked off by Jack Train and his disallowed peony and followed by Dimbleby and Harding locking horns verbally . . . while the dispersing studio audience refused to heed the pleas of the uniformed officials to disperse more quickly, preferring to stay on to listen to the free fight.

Writing of that night, Harding made no mention of the fracas after the transmission, merely saying: 'I make no other comment than to say that I was suspended from *Twenty Questions* for several months.' He did not add that the top brass at Broadcasting House took such a serious view of the matter that he was rusticated also from all the other programmes he was on at that time, including *Round Britain Quiz*.

He spent the early part of his banishment in a quiet hideaway in

Scotland. Mrs Sally Wright remembers that at her home in Crail, a small coastal towm in Fife, she received a surprise telegram from him one morning, two days after the rumpus on *Twenty Questions*. It read, simply: ARRIVING FOUR O'CLOCK THIS AFTERNOON.

The Wrights did not know Gilbert all that well. Mrs Wright had first met him during his Canadian phase, when she and her husband, who was with the RAF stationed in Canada, had been asked to join him on a round-the-Commonwealth Christmas broadcast. They had met him again in London, in the BBC club at the Bolivar, in what turned out to be the week preceding the *Twenty Questions* shambles. They had said, as people do when renewing acquaintance, 'If you ever happen to be up near Crail, do drop in and see us.'

When the storm broke after the BBC announced they were taking him off the air, his phone was going all day and newspapermen were besieging his flat, 'Crail' clicked in his mind as the ideal place to which to escape for a while. Which resulted in the telegram and his precipitous arrival at the Wright home in the hitherto dreamy little seaside town.

It was a bit awkward for Mrs Wright, since her husband had gone off to Germany on R.A.F. duty and her son was at boarding school in Edinburgh and she was alone in the house – but now not alone, now with the unpredictable Gilbert Harding.

'He paced the living room floor in deep gloom,' she recalls, 'his head down and his shoulders hunched, saying over and over again "I'll never get any more work, this is the end for me." He became more and more downcast and seemingly suicidal as the Scotch which I provided for him, wisely or unwisely, seemed to have the opposite effect to lifting him from his depression.

'Then suddenly he seemed to get hold of himself. He stood erect and said graciously, "I humbly apologise, dear Sally. It is unforgivable for me to inflict myself on you in this way. I shall take a sleeping pill and retire." Then, apologising abjectly again, he went out of the room.'

Either the sleeping pill failed to take effect or he did not take one, because he did not appear again until the early hours of the morning. At the house, that is. He had gone, not to bed, but into the town, where his steps had taken him unerringly to the popular pub in the high street. The arrival there, seemingly out of the blue, of Gilbert Harding in person, created a stir. All the solid drinkers of the town homed in on the pub. Mine host, with a fine disregard for the licensing laws, let things carry on until all hours and this was but the first of some memorable sessions during the five days Gilbert was there.

He cut a broad swathe through Crail and Sally Wright will tell you that even all these years afterwards the locals still talk about his visit there. The Wrights no longer have the house but whenever she goes back to Crail she is not long there before somebody invariably starts things off again with 'Remember the time Gilbert Harding came up here . . .'

When the success of *Twenty Questions* was at its height it was decided that there would be a separate overseas edition beamed to the Commonwealth countries. It would be chaired by Ted Kavanagh of ITMA fame, who happened to be a New Zealander, and the panellists would also be from the outposts of Empire. I became one of the team and we did the broadcasts from the Aeolian Hall in Bond Street, while the main show continued to go out from the Paris Cinema in Lower Regent Street. From time to time Richard Dimbleby would drop out of this to cover some Royal occasion and I would be called upon to take his place.

I remember arriving at the Paris Cinema for my first broadcast feeling quite excited about promotion to the First Division. The other panellists gave me a cool reception, in the radio-TV tradition of 'Never be helpful to a newcomer – he could do you out of your job.' Harding, on the other hand, greeted me warmly.

I had not met him since I had bumped into him outside Broadcasting House after the BBC had fired him from the staff and he had been dejected about his prospects as a free lance broadcaster. Now at the Paris Cinema we chatted about our times in Canada, he showed me around the set-up of the studio and in all ways made me welcome.

I had learned that as regards the regular panellists – Richard Dimbleby, Jack Train, Anona Winn and Joy Adamson – he had his own reasons for disliking them individually and as a team. Jack Train's constant stream of weak and contrived puns infuriated him. Apparently before one of the programmes Jack Train approached the producer and said: 'I want to use the question "Can it be found in a bird sanctuary?" Would that fit in with any of the objects tonight?'

'Jack,' said the producer, 'you know I can't tell you anything about the objects.'

'But I want to use "Can it be found in a bird sanctuary?" '

'Why?'

'You'll see,' said Train, with his well known grin.

'All right. Object number four. You could probably use it there.'

'Good!' said Train.

When the programme went on the air and number four duly came up, Train asked: 'Could you find it in a bird sanctuary?'

'Yes,' said Gilbert.

'Sanctuary much,' said Train.

The groan from the studio audience was echoed by the seven million

50

listeners. A stale bun is unpalatable, but as nothing compared to a stale pun. Harding once became so irked by Train's shuttle service of laboured puns that he said to him: 'Punning is like masturbation. It brings pleasure only to the person who is doing it.'

Richard Dimbleby he alluded to as 'obsequious granite' and his pomposity drove Gilbert up the wall. 'Oh God, you're so pompous, Richard' he once burst out to the great man, unable to contain his feelings. Dimbleby, with a genuinely innocent look, replied: 'Do you really think I'm pompous?' To which Harding's comment was: 'To be pompous is bad enough but not to know, not to be conscious of it – that is unforgivable.'

Before a broadcast starts it is not unusual for performers to visit the washroom for what is known as 'the nervous pee'. At the Paris Cinema I was going through that ritual when Harding came in. In the seclusion away from the rest of the team he starting consulting his clipboard, apparently checking the answers. Without looking at me but loud enough for me to hear, he said: 'The answer to Number 3 is Such-and-Such . . . the answer to Number 7 is So-and-So . . .'

'No, Gilbert,' I had to say to him. 'I know you can't abide the others and want me to show up well against them, but I'd rather take my own chances.'

Apart from the ethics of the thing, knowing answers beforehand presents a difficulty. You have to be a good actor to put it across properly – simulate the fumbling in one's mind, convincingly lead up to the triumphant announcement of the correct answer. Having an answer beforehand is for experienced actors only and, in point of fact, it is rare for panellists to know ahead of time . . . except for such lapses as Gilbert trying to do me a good turn.

We took our places in the studio proper and the show got under way, and Harding was seen to be loosening his collar and mopping perspiration from his brow. It was an extremely cold night outside and not all that warm in the theatre but he kept commenting to the audience, 'How can you stand this heat?' The truth of the matter was that brandy was exuding from every pore of his bulky frame.

He was to confess to me later that his problem with regard to drinking and performing was that early in his career he had had a stiff brandy before a broadcast and had done extremely well. 'I reasoned,' he said, 'that if I did well after one brandy I'd do twice as well if I had two. Two became three, three became four . . .' What number of brandies he had settled for as a regular routine I do not know, but he never went on the air unfortified.

At the conclusion of that first broadcast I did with him he did not join the others, to stand around and have the usual radio-TV 'How do you think we did?' post mortem. He grabbed hold of me and whisked me out to his waiting chauffeur-driven car. He did not say where we were going but soon the car pulled up outside one of the more fashionable and expensive Jermyn Street restaurants. At the bar, amid the 'Good evening, Mr Harding' chorus, he seemed disappointed at my having merely a simple lager. When we were at the table he pressed me to have the most elaborate, costly dishes. He seemed bent on being the lavish host. I could see that it was not through ostentation. He genuinely wanted to give me a memorable meal. Why me?

The reason seemed clear when he had dropped me off in the car and was being driven away and I saw him slumped down there in the back seat – a rich, successful, lonely man.

CHAPTER 8

A PRODUCT OF THE 1950s

Gilbert Harding's period of being 'the most famous man in Britain' neatly straddled the 1950s – from the dreary start of the decade when such things as clothes, sweets and petrol were still rationed to the advent of the more lively 1960s with the launching of the mini car, the hoisting of the mini skirt and *Lady Chatterley* winning her court case and ushering in the Permissive Age. He first earned for himself the name of 'Mr Rude' in November 1950 when on the *We Beg To Differ* show he told Dr Edith Summerskill to 'mind your own business', which, as TV critic Philip Phillips wrote, 'jolted the BBC out of its gentility' and was followed by a succession of headlines on the theme of ANOTHER HARDING RUMPUS right through until his death in November 1960.

There was no doubt that the 1950s were in need of someone to brighten them and perhaps it was the very drabness of the decade – especially the early part – which had much to do with the public at large taking Gilbert to their hearts and making him the most talked about personality of the time.

As the 1950s began the country was still referred to as 'poor, dear threadbare Britain', which was literally so with nobody being able to do very much about renewing their wardrobes (those ghastly Utility suits!), with their meagre supply of clothes coupons, and the shabby look extended to weed-strewn bomb sites and war damaged and delapidated buildings which could not be fixed up because the wartime restriction of work permits for both demolition and construction persisted well into the decade.

As well as clothes, sweets and petrol, other items such as tea, soap and sugar still required coupons. All food rationing did not end until July, 1954. Whisky was not rationed simply because there was not enough of it around to be rationed. Suspicious looking brands of the Glen Harpic type were to be had on the black market – for £5 a bottle, a price to which not even today's inflation has driven it.

People worried terribly about World War III, which was imminent, if one judged by the advertisements for purpose-built family bomb shelters and the Ban the Bomb marches organised by such people as Bertrand Russell.

Princess Margaret was having a bad time of it at the Palace, through doing the same thing her uncle had done in the 1930s – announcing she wanted to marry a divorced person. But Buckingham Palace and Canterbury were adamant and the answer was no.

Sad for Margaret, having to give up Peter Townsend, but even sadder news for everybody when her father died. At the funeral of George VI, Richard Dimbleby showed himself to be masterly in the covering of such solemn Royal occasions. Lyons, the caterers, were then running an advertising campaign which featured the slogan 'Where's George? He's gone to Lyonch!' It was obliterated from all hoardings along the route of King George's funeral, lined by hundreds of thousands of mourners.

At the start of the 1950s the Labour party had been in power. Attlee, Bevin and Bevan, Sir Stafford ('Christ and Carrots') Cripps, Herbert Morrison, seemingly dedicated to ensuring that grey would be the predominant colour in the already drab tapestry of Britain in the 1950s. It was no wonder that the general public seized upon anything, no matter how trivial, as a diversion from being told to tighten their belts and suffer in silence disastrous nationalisation. Brumas, the lovable bear at London zoo, was so headlined and publicised that those who flocked to watch his antics formed the longest queues ever seen in Regent's Park. Foreign visitors to England (few of them American tourists, since they were told by U.S. travel agents to avoid Britain – 'it's drearsville') were surprised to see on the front pages of the national newspapers the blown-up picture of a man's knee, also blown up. How could a man's knee be of such nationwide importance? They did not realise. It was Compton's knee. Would Denis Compton be fit for the forthcoming Tests against Australia? That was something with which the public at large could concern themselves. And of course so, too, were the ructions caused by the verbal broadsides and the indiscretions of Gilbert Harding on the television screen – in *What's My Line?* – and off it . . .

It was Harding who originated the term 'Auntie' for the BBC. It must be remembered that when he was first taken on by the BBC in 1939, the Corporation had merely been in its teens but by 1952 the smug, Establishment aura that had engulfed it so infuriated Harding that he was prompted to announce to the press that 'I will not have the BBC giving the impression of being a face-slapping auntie.'

What had given rise to this was his comment to one of the guests on *What's My Line?* It was Mr William Preston, who had challenged the panel – Harding, Elizabeth Allan, Lesley Storm and Jimmy Edwards – to guess his occupation of whisky broker. His manner of answering questions irritated Gilbert and eventually he said: 'I'm tired of looking at you.' This resulted in the headline next morning: HARDING IN TROUBLE AGAIN. Interviewed by the papers, Mr Preston said how deeply hurt he had been not to have received any sort of apology as he left the studio. 'And to think,' he added, 'that I had brought each of them a bottle of whisky.'

To people now it may seem to have all been very trivial, such a palaver over a rude remark to a challenger, but before Gilbert Harding came along nobody had dared to be so 'outspoken' on the BBC. The Corporation insisted that he make his apology to the whisky broker in the next edition of *What's My Line?* and the *Daily Express* was able to carry the banner headline: HARDING APOLOGISES AS 3,000,000 WATCH.

He was seen to be humble in his delivery of the apology. But he was not contrite. Within two weeks he was back on the 'Auntie' theme. On the radio programme *We Beg To Differ* he said: 'The BBC is a bearded and moustached auntie of a monopolistic corporation. Why there should be a passion for it passes my understanding.'

Considering the fact that he said that on a BBC programme it would seem to have been a fouling of his nest, and a dangerous thing for any broadcaster to do. At that time, and up to the advent of commercial television in 1955, a radio or television performer in Britain either worked for the BBC or didn't work at all. There was no other nest to go to. If you incurred the displeasure of Auntie you were out, just as Harding had been 'rested' following an outburst on *Twenty Questions* in 1951. Presumably after his second forthright jibe at his employers he would be taken off the air. But by then Gilbert Harding was becoming too big – 'the most listened to, most looked at man in Britain' – for them to do anything about it. The BBC dared not incur the wrath of his huge following.

His ability to make the headlines extended beyond his television and radio appearances. Another 'Harding rumpus' was created when he was invited to the Red Lion Hotel, Hounslow, to the annual dinner of the local magistrates. With his interest in Law, he had been quite looking forward to this dinner and was disappointed when he found that there were only three magistrates among more than a hundred guests for whom it was just a good excuse for a night out wining and dining. He exploded.

'I have been dragged along to this third-rate place, to a third-rate dinner for third-rate people.' he announced.

The press, always interested in a good Harding quote, got another from him as he was about to leave the scene of the upheaval he had created. 'A horrible evening, just another suburban do, and I was asked as Exhibit A,' he said, waving his invitation card. The incident received so much publicity that the brewers who owned the hotel felt forced to demand – and got – a printed apology from Gilbert.

In June 1953 the *Daily Sketch* carried a headline: STOP HARDING'S RUDENESS; THE JOKE IS OVER. Which of course gave them the chance to list all the Harding broadsides which had made news up to that time, for the further enjoyment of their readers.

Pubs and restaurants were most commonly the venues of Harding disturbances and an odd outcome of this was that often when he had a meal somewhere and everything had gone off without incident he would find that no bill was presented when he was about to leave. 'There is no charge, Mr Harding,' he would be told. 'We look forward to you coming in again.'

They really did look forward to him coming in again – and next time creating a disturbance sufficient to attract the press, with resultant good publicity. There is no really bad publicity for a restaurant, apart from the finding of too many empty Kittie-Kat tins in their garbage.

However, the absence of bills from restaurants was a matter of concern to Harding's accountant. With all the drawbacks to life in the 1950s, there was one glorious aspect. 'Entertaining' in the broadest sense, could be – and was, on a vast scale – listed as a deductable expense for income tax purposes, if you had the bills to prove it. The accountant brought the matter up with Gilbert and a few days later he came into the office and deposited on the accountant's desk several pads of blank bills from the then fashionable Trocadero restaurant in Shaftesbury Avenue.

'There you are,' said Gilbert. 'Fill them in yourself.'

The latter part of the 1950s was enlivened by what could only be called the Television Explosion. It would be an exaggeration to say that Gilbert Harding's progress from radio's *Twenty Questions* to *What's My Line?* in television was the cause of it but there was no doubt that he was at the forefront of the dramatic switch by the general public from radio listening to TV-viewing.

John Montgomery in his book *The Fifties* wrote: ' "Did you see Gilbert Harding on *What's My Line?*" was now the conversational opening gambit on the morning train, and in the office. If you had no telly in the front room you were out of things. It was the new status symbol.'

Older people tend to forget and the younger generation would hardly credit that in the latter part of the 1940s and even into the early 1950s

56

families were still sitting around the radio set in the living room of an evening as they assemble around the TV set today. Those bulky wireless sets with fretwork design over the netting where the sound came out were still as much a part of the furnishings as the three-piece suite, the tasselled lampshades and Canadian geese flying across the wall. If you were posh – or Dad had made a killing on the black market during the war – you had a 'radiogram', a term which served the twin purpose of defining a cable received at sea and a combination wireless set and gramophone. But whichever it was, it was the focal point of the family's evening entertainment – even more so than the television set is nowadays.

There were two main reasons why that was so.

First of all, transistor radios were still a long way off; the whole family hooked themselves into the big wireless in the main room and did not go their separate ways to listen to their own favourite programmes on a 'tranny'. The Bell Telephone Company developed the transistor in the States in 1948 but it was used in the 1950s primarily for tele-communications and did not make its full impact on radio listening until the 1960s. There *were* portable radios in the old days but they were cumbersome and voracious of batteries. Harding, in fact, had a Pye portable in grey sharkskin 'leatherette' that was the size of a woman's vanity case.

A second reason why the big wireless set was even more a of family attraction than the 'telly' now was that although teenagers as a separate social group had existed in the States since the 1930s, in Britain they were only just starting to be siphoned off from the rest of the family. 'The British family' was still a tightly knit unit. Teenage members of the family did not go off to pursue their own interests as they do now – they sat with Mum and Dad and listened to *Meet the Huggetts, Dick Barton, Twenty Questions, Ray's a Laugh, Take it From Here, Life With the Lyons* and *Family Favourites*.

It was small wonder that folk were still radio orientated because even for those who did own a TV set there was not much to view at the start of the 1950s compared to what was offered on radio. From 6.30 a.m. to midnight there was always something to listen to on the Home Service, the Light Programme and the Third Programme, not to mention the original pirate stations, Radio Luxembourg and Radio Athlone (if you could pick up their rather patchy transmission). But television, restarted in July 1946 after its wartime blackout, was still very thin indeed, as epitomised by this two-line listing in *The Times* of all the programmes for a typical Sunday evening in 1950:

5 p.m. For the Children. 8. Weekly Review. 8.15 Comedy: 'Square Pegs'. 9.45 News (sound only).

A little unfair, perhaps, to choose Sunday as an example, since the BBC were then still rather self-conscious about being too entertaining on the Sabbath. But during the week any daytime telecasting was almost exclusively devoted to sport (racing, a Test Match, Wimbledon) and evening viewing from 7 to 10 p.m. on a single black-and-white channel was no great inducement to go to the expense of buying a television set.

Radio-TV licences in 1951, when *What's My Line?* made its debut, stood at 736,941. The number of television sets sold in 1953 was 1,600,000. By 1955, when Commercial TV started, this figure had jumped to 4,000,000. In 1959 – 10,000,000!

Television emptied the cinemas. Attendance at the picture theatres in 1951 was 1,365,000,000, but by 1959 this had nosedived to 601,000,000 – more than cut in half. More than one in four cinemas had closed or switched to bingo. Some were converted to accommodate another aspect of American fashion, so prevalent in the 1950s. But ten-pin bowling, despite all the money and effort devoted to trying to promote it, failed to catch on with the British.

Just as the predicted demise of the theatre when the new 'talkies' arrived in the 1930s did not take place, live theatre proved too hardy to be killed off by television. A reason for this was that television showed itself at the outset, slow in evolving something which is a pure 'television play', i.e. drama of and for TV and no other medium.

However, one branch of the theatre was all but killed stone dead by the advent of television – music hall. How could any but the top variety theatres such as the London Palladium compete with the entertainment to be had on TV in one's own home? Suburban music halls like the Met in Edgware Road and those in the provinces fought for survival by giving the public what they could not get on television – nudes. Managers in the provinces vied with one another in thinking up suggestive titles for their shows. One of them who billed his attraction 'This Is The Show', with each capital letter in brightly lit neon, found himself in court.

Television caused a revolution in the Englishman's drinking habits. It emptied the pubs – the public bars, that is to say, not the saloon bars, most of whose customers felt it was a mark of social and intellectual superiority not to be 'glued to the idiot box'. One licensee in Warley, Essex, was quoted in the press as saying: 'We have an army camp nearby and even the soldiers stationed there prefer the sight of Gilbert Harding on their camp TV set to a pint of bitter with me. Anything that'll stop a soldier from getting the hell out of camp when he has the chance *must* be compulsive viewing.' Public bar trade dwindled to such an extent that publicans pulled down the dividing wall between working class customers and their 'betters' and class distinction in public houses was at an end with the coming of the all-one-bar pub we know today.

There was much bemoaning of the fact that television would kill conversation as a form of social intercourse – who would dare to try to talk while everyone else was engrossed in *Beat the Clock* on *Sunday Night at the London Palladium*? And even today those who want to chat get short shrift from those who want to watch. But oddly enough one of the things which was thought to have been most vulnerable to television – the reading of books – did not receive a body blow. In fact quite the reverse was the case.

At the start of the 1950s, when TV was merely a few hours mainly in the evening and only on one channel, the annual borrowings at the public libraries were around 300-million. By the end of the 1950s, with another channel and much daytime telecasting, this figure had risen to over 400-million. Why? One reason was that since television kept people at home instead of going out for entertainment it was logical to have a library book handy for something to do when *not* watching the box. But the main reason was that TV could not help but be educational to the extent not only of stimulating interest in books on which certain programmes were based but also a general desire to read about people and places and things viewers became exposed to on the box.

Gilbert Harding, however, was never caught up in this 'reading bulge'. In fact, for one who would not have minded being regarded as an intellectual, reading had little part in his mature life. Alan Melville, his close neighbour in Brighton, once remarked to Gilbert on the absence of books around his home. Gilbert led him to a cupboard where he was able to show Melville that he did indeed own some.

Brian Masters, who spent much time at Gilbert's London flat in the latter years of his life, said: 'There were no books in the flat. He never did any reading. He felt he had done all his basic reading many years ago. He knew much of Trollope, Jane Austen, Dickens off by heart, thanks to his photographic memory, which he had from infancy. Apparently his mother used to re-read to him his favourite nursery rhymes and children's stories and even before he could read himself he used to correct her if she made a mistake or skipped a bit. He used to recite to me long passages of Dickens and other authors he admired. He once did a whole act of *Hamlet*, taking all the parts. But instead of reading he used to sit and drink and watch television.'

Noel Coward's attitude – 'Television is not for watching, it is for appearing on' – was not one which Gilbert went along with. Such was his TV addiction towards the end of his life that he used to watch two sets at once to avoid the risk of missing anything. 'He would sit there with his drink,' Masters said, 'watching television and arguing with it.

He would carry on these one-way discussions with whoever it was he happened to be watching and get quite violent about it. I remember him having a set-to like that with Cliff Michelmore, who was big in those days as the original *Tonight* man, and then when the programme was finished he phoned up Michelmore and continued the argument in person. Not that he was always critical. He very much admired the acting of Peter Cushing, for example.'

Television plays were always live in those days and Peter Cushing remembers: 'After each programme Gilbert Harding never failed to ring up to express his pleasure and be most generous with his praise. When I appeared as the mystery personality on *What's My Line?* it was even more kind and generous of him to say how deeply impressed he had been by my performance in the adaptation of Orwell's "1984" – before the huge audience of that panel game.'

Huge audience indeed, always somewhere between 3 and 4 million, which was in the top bracket for those times. Throughout the television explosion of the 1950s the BBC were pleased to be able to report each year in their Handbook that *What's My Line?* was at the head of or in the top three of the list of their most popular programmes.

Harding as millions of viewers were accustomed to see him, an unpredictable volcano.

Gilbert Harding photographed with his pekinese Cham-pu, 1956.

Gilbert Harding with his sister on his father's knee.

Nine-year-old Gilbert in his blue coat school uniform with his sister.

Harding at Cambridge: "To my surprise I found myself making
friends." He is in the centre of the back row.

Learning his trade as a BBC interviewer, Harding visits an R.A.F. training centre during the war.

We Beg To Differ, 1951. The male's viewpoint from Gilbert Harding and Bernard Braden. The female's from Barbara Kelly, Barbara Mullen, Gladys Young and Joan Greenwood. Pat Dixon at the table.

A shot of the *What's My Line* team in action, with Harding, Elizabeth Allen, Jerry Desmonde, and the

Harding in hospital being visited by Anona Winn and Elizabeth Allan.

Harding chairs a Twenty Questions session. The panel consists of: Jack Train, Anona Winn, Joy Adamson,

Harding as a baby with his mother. "I owe my chance in the world to my mother".

The adult Gilbert Harding with his ageing mother at a school prizegiving.

Three studies of Gilbert Harding taken during the famous *Face to Face* programme with John Freeman during which he broke down as he recalled the death of his mother.

On the verandah of his Brighton home, 1956.

As seen by Nicholas Bentley.

The autograph. "At the going rate," observed Harding dourly as he signed three autographs for a small boy, "for three of these you should be able to get one of Tommy Steele's".

CHAPTER 9

WHAT'S MY LINE?

Gilbert Harding described how he made his debut on television:

One overcast evening towards the end of May, 1951, I drove to the BBC's new television studios at Lime Grove, Shepherd's Bush. I had been invited to see the telefilm of a new quiz that had just been flown over from the United States. Having already heard an unimpressive sound recording of this show, I arrived at the studios convinced that I was wasting my time.

The lights dimmed and the screen lit up with a picture of four grim-looking Americans gazing biliously at a Question Master. After some preliminary chit-chat a muscular representative of the American industrial classes appeared and, unaided by any preliminary mime, the four gloomy members of the panel began making attempts to guess the muscular one's occupation. It seemed extremely dreary to me and I cannot remember much more about the telefilm because I almost fell asleep in my chair.

Up went the lights again and we began to discuss what some of us had seen. Suddenly I brightened. I thought there might be possibilities, after all. What had bothered me about the film was the manifest puerility of four adults trying to guess a person's job – and invariably a pretty boring job, at that. Now it seemed to me that everything rested on the Question Master's insight. As long as he did not take these jobs too seriously the whole thing could flare up into a spirited, good-natured parlour affair on the lines of Twenty Questions. *So when Waldman asked for my opinion I told him I thought there were possibilities – if I could be Question Master.*

As I invariably do, I seemed to have put my foot into things. It soon became clear that I had not been under consideration for the rôle of Question Master, only as a possible for the panel.

What Harding did not mention was that the commercials had been left in the telerecording. The show was sponsored in the States by Stopette, a brand of deodorant spray, and there were three breaks for plugs for the product, one of which featured the firms' main slogan – 'Make your arm-pit your charm-pit.' This brought hoots of laughter from the little assembly of officials and performers of the BBC monopoly. How typical of the way they did things in America! Thank heaven that British broadcasting would never, ever be sullied by commercial plugs . . .

After the screening several weeks elapsed during which Gilbert heard nothing further. He was not unduly worried, since he had plenty on his plate with *Twenty Questions*, *Round Britain Quiz* and *We Beg To Differ*. He was finding work strenuous enough without tackling another job, and in a field other than radio. He felt satisfied enough with the progress he had made as a broadcaster. He felt he had mastered the microphone, was it really necessary to go on to television?

One of the main reasons for the delay in the decision by the planners as to whether or not to put on *What's My Line?* was that they had had their minds set on Eamonn Andrews for the chairman. Gilbert had indeed rather thrown a spanner in the works. Although not yet the big name he was to become he did have some reputation as a question master on radio and was certainly much better known to the British public than the younger man from Ireland. So when Ronnie Waldman got in touch with him to tell him that a compromise had been reached he was prepared to listen, since after all he was a newcomer to television. The deal was that Eamonn would be chairman for the first programme and he would follow in the next, and he agreed that that was fair enough.

The British version of *What's My Line?* was launched on July 16 1951. In the *Radio Times* for that week it was introduced by a little feature hidden away in one corner, headed 'Something New in Quiz Games' and concluding 'The programme, one way and another, looks like being a lot of fun.'

The producer was T. Leslie Jackson, popularly known as Jacko, who was the same age as Harding and had been brought up in Ireland, where he had studied at the Abbey Theatre. Jackson had got a job as a studio manager with the BBC at the restart of television in 1946 and his first excursion into production was with the comedy series *An Evening at Home with the Bradens*, which did not catch on, to be followed by *What's My Line?*, which certainly did.

It was one of the TV shows responsible for emptying the pubs and, when it was switched from mid-week to Sunday, it severely interfered with church attendance.

Was Gilbert the whole show? Dicky Leeman, who took over from Jackson later in its run, wrote: 'When each *What's My Line?* had been viewed and debated, there followed on Monday mornings an airing in public on trains and buses, at offices, in pubs and cafes. . . . There had never been a talking point like the virtues or vices, alleged or real, of this modern Dr Johnson.'

For those unfamiliar with the most popular quiz show ever televised in Britain or the United States, where it ran for seventeen years, this was the format of *What's My Line?*

A challenger would sign in by writing his name on a blackboard. He would then do a piece of mime of something he did in connection with his job. While the panel of two men and two women did their best to interpret this, the challenger would join the chairman at his desk opposite the panellists. Then each panellist in turn would question him about his job with what came to be standard queries designed to get maximum information in the quickest way, such as: Are you self-employed? Do you provide a service? Can your job be done by both men and women? Is there an end product? Is it smaller than a football, larger than a motor car?

On the chairman's desk was a stand with numbers up to 10, which could be folded over one by one and revealed to the audience. As long as a panellist received an answer of 'Yes' to his questions, he continued, but if he got a 'No' the chairman would turn a number over and the questioning would move to the next panellist. Any challenger able to score 10 'No's' would be deemed to have beaten the panel and he would be given a diploma to record the event. (Such diplomas are still to be seen framed on the walls of homes throughout the country, like doctor's diplomas in waiting rooms.)

After each challenger had finished, whether he had won or not, he would be interviewed by the chairman and there would be general chit-chat with members of the panel about his work. If there *was* an end product, the challenger would usually give each of them a sample.

To give the show a change of pace, about halfway through a Mystery Celebrity would be the challenger. The panellists would don blindfolds and the celebrity would do his best to disguise his voice.

The first panel consisted of Marghanita Laski, Barbara Kelly, Ted Kavanagh and Jerry Desmonde, who had been straight man to comedian Sid Field. The plan of having Eamonn and Gilbert alternating as chairman was short-lived. When Gilbert took over for the second edition it proved to be a disaster – through no fault of his. The call-boy, who had to send on each challenger after his occupation had been announced to the viewers and the audience, made a mistake. Gilbert, as chairman, was of course also in the know but instead of it being a Male Nurse, it was a Panel Beater who took his place alongside Gilbert.

The trouble began when the challenger was asked 'Has your job anything to do with transport?'

'Yes,' said the Panel Beater, whose job after all was to straighten out dents in the bodywork of motor vehicles.

'No, it hasn't,' corrected Gilbert, thinking in terms of a Male Nurse.

And so the questioning went on in complete confusion until the Panel Beater, naturally enough in the circumstances, wound up un-identified by the panel.

'He's a Male Nurse,' announced Gilbert.

'No, I'm not. I'm a Panel Beater.'

'Oh, are you?' said Gilbert. 'I don't know what the devil's happening, but this is probably the last time I shall appear on TV.'

As so often happens in a cock-up of that nature the guiltless person at the focal point of it is made the scapegoat. It certainly did look as though it was Gilbert's exit from television, definitely in regard to chairmanship of *What's My Line?* at least. It was Eamonn's job from then on.

Leeman, the producer, writing shortly afterwards: 'And what, do you suppose, did Eamonn Andrews think about that little misunder-standing? Alas, he was in Skegness doing a concert; so he missed it. He says with a twinkle in his eye that it almost broke his heart.'

However, for the fifth programme it was decided to drop Ted Kavanagh and give Gilbert a try on the panel, and subsequently as other panellists were chopped and changed, that seat on the end was permanently his. It made him. His presence on the panel made *What's My Line?* It had not got good reviews at its opening and it was not until he got into his stride that it gained any impetus.

Of the original panel Jerry Desmonde was retained and was to be Gilbert's running mate during its early days. But Marghanita Laski wanted no more of it after its first broadcast. She had been brought on to the show because Leslie Jackson liked her articles in the *Observer* and Ronnie Waldman, Head of Light Entertainment, was similarly enthusiastic about her, having known her when they were both at Oxford. In due course we will deal with Marghanita Laski's reaction against the 'instant fame of being a TV face' but suffice to say here that it was only after much coaxing from Jackson and Waldman that she could be lured back for other appearances.

Barbara Kelly was also disturbed by her success on *What's My Line*. She had set out with husband Bernie Braden from Canada for England in the winter of 1949-50. Just prior to leaving she had had her front teeth capped in anticipation of TV close-ups, but television had not been the Braden's primary target. Resentful of the quip that 'the only culture Canada has is agriculture', their aim had been to gain experience and make their name on the London stage and then return to establish Theatre in Canada.

Bernie had managed to get the important part of the gauche lover of Blanche (played by Vivien Leigh) in the West End version of *A Streetcar Named Desire* and Barbara was to say: 'I know jolly well that appearances on *What's My Line?* contributed to my being chosen for the West End play, *Angels in Love*.' They had one or two other minor engagements but success on the London stage eluded them. So it was a matter of their turning to radio comedy, in which Bernie had done well in Canada. British radio listeners took *Bedtime With Braden* to their hearts. His reputation on this side of the Atlantic was established – as a radio comedian. Barbara did some comedy shows with him, reluctantly, still holding out for the elusive stage career.

Meanwhile, having been on the panel for the first airing of *What's My Line?* in 1951, she was tried again in November 1952, and became a permanent fixture. Dicky Leeman said of her: 'Her racy, worldly style and her slick wit kept her bubbling like the best and gayest of champagne.'

The challengers on the first edition were a Street Trader, a Chauffeuse, a Cocktail Shaker and a Swimming Instructress. Subsequently the jobs were a mixture of the straightforward, the unusual and the out-landish. Everyday occupations like Taxi Driver, Barber, Receptionist, Schoolmistress were not necessarily easy for the panel. All four of those they failed to guess. And by the same token unusual jobs did not always prove difficult to track down. They got Chicken Sexer, Confetti Cutter, Maggot Breeder and Handcuff Maker, and Isobel Barnett, being a doctor, had no trouble at all with Electroencephalographer (operator of brain wave recording machine). But they *were* baffled by Catherine Wheel Winder, Pepperpot Perforator, Tennis Ball Inflater, Jig-saw Puzzle Cutter, Jelly Baby Varnisher, Flint Knapper, Hog Slapper, Micropalaeontologist (one who studies micro-fossils).

Since each challenger was interviewed after the guessing was over this always added interest to the programme, and prolonged the Monday morning chat in the office about what had been on *What's My Line?* on Sunday night. The Onion Peeler, for instance, Mrs Mary Downie from Edinburgh . . . 'Isn't it amazing that she's been peeling 500 onions a day for fourteen years without shedding a single tear! Apparently the secret is that if you soak the onion in brine beforehand you won't cry.'

The challenger who was a Ship's Captain, on one of the big trans-atlantic liners, told of a girl who was at his table who was very attractive but so shy that nobody could get very much out of her. However, when they were coming into rough weather and the stewards started damp-ening the tablecloths in the dining saloon she asked why they were doing that.

'It's to stop the knives and forks and things from rolling around.' the Captain explained to her.

'Oh,' she said brightly. 'I must remember to wet the bed tonight.'

But of course the challenger who was the classic, the one who had everybody talking not just on the Monday morning but for a long time afterwards, was the Sagger Maker's Bottom Knocker. A Mr Adams, of the firm of John Sadler & Sons in Burslem, became a nationally known figure through the job he did for them. A sagger, it seems, is a receptacle in which china is baked and part of the process requires a skilled knocking off of the bottom of it.

Challengers could benefit greatly by the publicity they received, especially if they were self-employed and their 'end product' took the viewer's fancy. More than one was launched on a highly successful career.

There was a singer who had a very moving effect on the the viewing public. On the face of it, it seemed an ordinary enough challenge. When the producer's secretary had displayed the placard to the audience giving his occupation as a Ballad Singer, he went and took his seat beside Eamonn. He managed to get a tally of 10 'No's' and was duly presented with his diploma for beating the panel.

It was then that Gilbert Harding said to him: 'Excuse me, sir. Have you had the misfortune to lose your sight?' It was not until then that those watching learned that Gerry Brereton was indeed totally blind, having lost his sight on a Commando raid during the war. When he had been suggested by his manager, Teddy Sommerfield, as a possible challenger Leslie Jackson had been doubtful.

'Just think of the risk,' he had said. 'Supposing he should trip on that step down from the back of the set or the other things that could go wrong.'

Sommerfield, knowing his protege so well, said, 'Try him out and see.'

'All right, bring him along one Sunday afternoon and if it's workable I'll use him on that night's show.'

'It won't be necessary for me to come,' said Sommerfield.

When Brereton appeared, alone, at Jackson's office he was amazed that he seemed to look directly at him when he spoke and gave no hint that he was blind. Jackson took him to the studio set and holding him firmly by one arm took him right through the routine of his entrance, up four steps to the archway at the back of the set, across to the signing-in board, down one step and then to Eamonn's desk and to the seat beside the chairman's.

'Now let's do it again,' said Jackson. 'I'll hold your arm.'

'You won't need to,' said Brereton. He told Jackson that he had memorised how many steps there were up and down, at what angle he had to turn and how many paces he had to take as he made his way to the challenger's chair. 'Would you like me to do it?' He went through the whole sequence by himself like any normal person, while Jackson and studio technicians watched in amazement. And that night on the show he did it all again just as faultlessly.

His appearance on *What's My Line?* brought a flood of engagements and a recording contract. He became a pop star of the 1950s and his name was included in the line-up for the next Royal Command Variety Performance.

Nowadays it is remarked how celebrities jostle to get on the Muppets show or that of Morecambe and Wise. This using of a popular TV show as a shop window was old stuff to *What's My Line?* Notables of all types made no bones about letting it be known that they were available for the mystery spot and the producer's phone rang incessantly with theatrical agents trying to get their clients on.

The celebrity on the first ever transmission was Alec Bedser, who was in the midst of demolishing South Africa in the Tests of that season. Or rather, it was intended that he alone would appear. But Eric tagged along with his illustrious brother, and it was literally a twin appearance.

From then on there was a formidable list of assorted celebrities of lasting and passing fame such as Sir John Barbirolli, coloured sprinter McDonald Bailey ... Maurice Chevalier, who deceived the panel by using his normal voice instead of zat thick French arc-cent he ah-fect-ted on stage and screen ... Don Bradman, Sam Goldwyn, Bob Hope, who signed in as Bing Crosby ... the soft-loud pop pianist Charlie Kunz and Aussie concert pianist Eileen Joyce, ... Prince (I gotta Horse) Monolulu, Air Chief Marshal Lord Dowding, 'Mr Teasie-Weasie' ... Sharman Douglas, whose claim to fame was being daughter of the U.S. Ambassador and a member of the Princess Margaret set ... Kathy Beaumont (who she?), Norman Hartnell, Walt Disney, Gordon Pirie...

A slight problem about the celebrity spot was that if the panel failed to guess who it was, that implied that he or she was not all that famous, which would be rather a hurt to the vanity. So almost always the celebrity was identified, thanks to chairman Andrews dropping a few hints if the panel were fumbling. Occasionally, though, a mystery guest would beat the panel and the first to do so was a Spurs and England soccer player who appeared to be so inarticulate that the panellists were baffled. They were quite unable to identify Alf Ramsey.

Only once did the show go out without a guest celebrity. Randolph Turpin had been scheduled to appear but when the contact man went to the National Sporting Club to pick him up he was found to be so busy relaxing from the pressures of being a world champion boxer that he was in no fit state to go on the air.

After the programme had been running for three years there was a minor setback to the assertion that 'everybody' watched *What's My Line?*. When Roger Bannister agreed to be the guest he said: 'Could you please tell me what I'm supposed to do? I've never seen the programme.'

After Chris Chataway beat the Russian Kutz in the 5,000 metres at the White City in world record time producer Leeman let some time elapse before inviting him, to let things settle down following the explosion of national pride, otherwise the panel would have sensed at once who was the guest. Nevertheless Leeman was to write: 'Chris Chataway had the biggest reception from the audience I have ever heard in any show I have produced, and come to think of it, in any show I have seen.'

That was in 1955 and Leeman went on: 'I believe Chris Chataway could become a great TV personality when he decides to forsake athletics. Maybe he could blend a TV career with his profession in the brewing trade. He had charm, good looks, a quick, keen brain, wit and an essentially masculine, friendly appeal. What more could one want? If by chance he should try, I tip him for stardom in a new field.' On that track record, Leeman could have made a fortune as a racing tipster.

Maurice Winnick, as owner of the British rights of *What's My Line?*, saw to it that he had much to do with the production of the programme, which was not to the liking of those directly connected with it. Eamonn Andrews described him as 'hawk-faced, with a heavy temper and an accent that was an uneasy mixture of American drawl and London English. He was loud, aggressive and had a slightly contemptuous manner. He always seemed to imply he had more important things to do but would deal first with this trivial and unprofitable interruption.'

All did not run smoothly between Gilbert and Maurice Winnick. On one occasion Sophia Loren was the mystery guest. At that time she was not the internationally known star she is today. With Gina Lollabrigida she was merely one of a cluster of Italian glamour starlets who had been brought to London for publicity and the hope of breaking into the Big Time.

When she beat the panel and her name was announced it was clear that Gilbert had never heard of her. Eamonn Andrews, ever aquiver at what was likely to come out of Gilbert's corner, was obviously fearful of his rumblings developing into an explosion. But on the air Gilbert managed to constrain himself, reserving his outburst for Maurice Winnick after the show.

He buttonholed him and demanded to know why he brought on to the programme 'celebrities of whom we have never heard'.

'She was on the front page of the *Daily Mirror* a couple of days ago,' said Winnick.

'How did she achieve that?'

'She was married by proxy.'

'Am I to take it, then,' said Gilbert, 'that I am expected to keep myself informed about the sexual perambulations of the illiterate and the obscure?'

When *What's My Line?* had become firmly established – billed every week in the *Radio Times* as 'TV's Most Popular Programme' – a stage version was produced, opening at London's Adelphi Theatre in 1952 and then going on a provincial tour. Harding was headlined as THE MOST LOOKED-AT AND LISTENED-TO MAN IN BRITAIN, based on his *Twenty Questions* and *What's My Line?* broadcasts each week and twice-nightly theatre appearances.

Jack Hylton was the presenter of the stage show and undoubtedly he was the origin of the Hardingism 'He is such a snob he won't even ride in the same car with his chauffeur.' The bandleader of the 1930s turned impresario was at that time launching the singing career of a monumentally untalented young lady who was a close friend and Harding liked to tell the story of what had happened when Hylton and his protégé were being driven into the provinces to the venue of another of the fiascos. Hylton suddenly got the urge for fish and chips. 'Stop at the next town', he informed his chauffeur, 'and get some'. This having been done, they drove on into the country and stopped by the roadside to get out and enjoy the view while having their fish and chips. The car was a Rolls-Royce with old-fashioned running boards and as Hylton and the young lady seated themselves and started pecking through the newspaper wrappings the chauffeur made to sit down beside them. Hylton looked at him, shocked. 'Don't you know your place?' He said. 'Get around to the other side of the car.'

The *What's My Line?* television show had settled down to what was virtually a permanent team: Eamonn in the chair, with veterans Gilbert and Barbara Kelly, who had been joined by Isobel Barnett and David Nixon on the panel. There has been much shuffling with the female contingent, fostered in no small measure by feminine squabbles. Elizabeth Allan, British actress who had some success in Hollywood, had had a run on the panel, and others included Frances Day, Dorothy Dickson, Monica Dickens, Chislaine Alexander, Jill Craigie and Lesley Storm.

The unlikely advent of Lady Barnett had been occasioned by her appearance on radio's *Town Forum* from the Midland Region, where she lived in Leicester. One of these programmes was put out on television and the BBC planners, impressed by 'her charm, good looks and intelligence', felt she would do well on the *Line*.

When she first came to the studio Gilbert also was impressed. Perhaps to quite a degree by the title. 'Where Gilbert's concerned.' someone once said, 'a title is vital.' He assured everybody that 'I shall always refer to her as Lady Barnett, never Isobel.'

But her early appearances were hardly a success. She showed herself to be entirely inexperienced in that field – 'I felt like a goldfish swimming for my life in a tankful of pike,' as she put it – but that was forgivable. However, in addition she committed the sin of being dull, which on television is quite unforgivable. Feeling she would be gobbled up by the personalities and the experience of the pike, she could not relax. The TV critics showed her no mercy and the programme chiefs indicated she would have to be unloaded. Gilbert fought for the 'absolutely delightful' Lady Barnett to be retained and may have felt that his pleading had much to do with her not being dropped.

In point of fact what happened was that travelling up to London from Leicester for her fifth appearance she read a further batch of scathing comments about herself in the Sunday papers. She agreed with what was being written about her and realised the axe was imminent. So – her whole approach to that evening's session was 'I couldn't care less.' For the first time she let herself go. She was transformed – and 'the new Isobel Barnett' developed into the highly successful broadcaster we all know.

She and Gilbert got on very well, better than he hit it off with most of the others. As people, not performers, the two had much in common. Both in their separate ways did good works. Writing his weekly column for the *People*, he would phone the doctor-magistrate at her home to learn of deserving causes she had come across at hospitals and in the courts to which he could give helpful publicity. On the programme she would do her best, with a cautionary tap on his arm, to restrain him when he showed signs of a Harding outburst. In the hospitality room after the show when he would often sit alone being dejected about something or other, she would be the one who would go to him and chat him out of it.

A friend said of her: 'Isobel is one of the very few people I know who are genuinely as pleasant and charming as they appear to be.' She brought a lot of understanding and concern to the complex personality of Gilbert. She said, 'Nobody *liked* Gilbert. They either loved him or hated him.' She told of once when he was coming to stay with her and her family, her then young son Alistair, basing his reaction on the Harding image, said: 'Why doesn't he stay at a hotel? He'll just be cross with me and everybody else.' But after only ten minutes or so of exposure to the 'ogre' Gilbert Harding, 'they had become the staunchest of friends.'

She felt that Gilbert was so often wrongly branded as rude when on analysis he was really being put upon, and quite rightly, if ill-advisedly, gave vent to his annoyance. A typical example she cited was an incident at Crewe station when Gilbert was waiting for a connection and bumped into someone also waiting for a train whom he had not met since they had been boys together at the Wolverhampton school. They had only a few minutes to spare before Gilbert's train would take him in one direction and his school chum's the opposite way, but they had barely started on their nostalgic chat when a man approached Harding.

'You're Gilbert Harding, aren't you?'

A long-suffering 'yes' from Gilbert.

'My wife's sitting over there. She'd love to meet you.'

'I'm sorry but I've just met an old friend. We haven't much time. I *would* like to have a talk with him.'

'But my wife's one of your biggest fans. She'd be so disappointed . . .' etc. etc.

Gilbert consented under continuous pressure, determined to make it brief. The woman was sitting on one of the platform benches with her two sons. Gilbert spoke to the boys. Then he said to the man, 'Are they ill?'

'No. They're perfectly all right.'

'Oh,' said Gilbert. 'I thought they were paralysed.'

'Paralysed?'

'It is customary, is it not, for young people to stand up when addressed by an older person?'

'Paralysed!' the wife burst out. 'What an awful thing to say!'

'You're being very rude,' the husband said to Gilbert.

Turmoil. Four enemies made by Gilbert. Everybody would be told how they had met him and how awful he had been to them. Gilbert's friend, coming over and saying he had to dash for his train, unhappy. Gilbert unhappy at being denied a pleasant interlude with him.

Lady Barnett felt that although he could perhaps have been more diplomatic in his handling of the affair, was he really in the wrong in this instance? Emotionally and revealingly, for her, she concluded a piece she wrote about him when he died: 'I am going to miss so much his saying to me, "Fill up your glass, dear lady, and pay attention. You will not have heard this story." '

In 1954 David Nixon was not widely known, merely doing his particular type of magic and patter in cabaret and on children's shows. However, he got a call from Dicky Leeman and when he went to his office he was asked whether he would like to appear on *What's My Line?* He thought Leeman meant as a mystery guest and said it was not on because he knew Gilbert and he would have no difficulty in identifying him.

'I don't mean as a guest,' said Leeman. 'I mean on the panel.'

It seemed they were having a problem filling the other male spot on the panel, as support to Gilbert. Since Jerry Desmonde had become unavailable it had been regarded as the 'hot seat'. Various people had been tried out – including George Formby, Frankie Howerd, Wilfred Hyde White and Michael Dennison – without great success. The little known Nixon of those days felt flattered and was rather taken aback at being considered for the job. 'People today probably don't realise how important *What's My Line?* was. It was the biggest thing that ever hit show business.' The only experience he had had as a panellist was in an audition for a radio quiz that had not got off the ground. Would he really be capable of making a go of this?

As he and Leeman were discussing it the telephone went. It was someone at the *Radio Times*, they were going to press, they had to have the name of the fourth panelist. Leeman raised querying eyebrows in Nixon's direction. Wondering what he was letting himself in for, Nixon nodded.

As it transpired, what he was letting himself in for of course was instant fame. Appearing on *What's My Line?* made him. He carried it off so well that for the next six years, until Gilbert died in 1960 and the show petered out, he was very much the regular in that seat on the panel. His success on the programme brought better contracts in his own field, he was given TV shows of his own and rose to his present secure place in the entertainment world. For Nixon it all dates from that nod to Leeman in his office in 1954.

How had he and Gilbert got on together? 'Some people on the programme used to get impatient with him. I didn't. We spent a lot of time together. We talked a lot. I felt it was an important thing in my life, meeting Gilbert Harding. You couldn't be with him without something rubbing off. I feel privileged to have known him.'

Alan Melville said of Gilbert that he could be 'kind, gentle and sloppily sentimental'. David Nixon confirmed this when he told me of the days when *What's My Line?* used to go out from the theatre in Shepherd's Bush that had been converted for television. He was in Gilbert's dressing room before the show one evening when the sound came to them of a 'diabolically bad' trumpeter entertaining the queue outside. Gilbert called the floor manager and took out all the small change in his pocket and handed it to him. Nixon thought he was going to get the floor manager to ask the trumpeter to knock it off. Instead he said to him: 'Will you take this to the musician outside and ask him to play *Abide With Me?* In due course *Abide With Me* came through to them in the dressing room. Gilbert broke off his chat with Nixon and went and sat in a corner, soon to be dissolved in tears. It was shortly after the death of his mother. It had been her favourite hymn.

How were things between Gilbert and Eamonn Andrews? 'There was a stock gag among comedians in those days that went: I met this chap who had a black eye and I asked him "How did you get that black eye?" and he said "I walked between Gilbert Harding and Eamonn Andrews." That was rather an exaggeration, though.' But Gilbert and Eamonn were hardly the sort you would expect to see having a drink together in a pub. 'Encountered in a pub? A curt nod, that's what it would be.'

David Nixon said that the point was that 'Eamonn was strait-laced and was somewhat shocked at Gilbert's treatment of some of the people who came on the programme.'

It must be remembered that Eamonn Andrews was still in his twenties when he undertook the *What's My Line?* assignment and he was very much the new boy just over from Ireland.

He had been born in 1922 in Dublin in Synge Street, in which another Irishman besides Eamonn had been born who was to make a name for himself in England – Bernard Shaw. Eamonn made his first broadcast for Radio Eireann when only seventeen, doing a boxing commentary on the Amateur Championships in which he himself was competing, to emerge as the All-Ireland Amateur Middleweight Junior Champion. He built up a reputation for himself in Irish radio not only as a boxing commentator but also as an interviewer and quiz show performer. He did some work for the BBC and in 1950 took the adventurous step of deciding to move permanently to London. He expressed himself as being 'frightened at the prospect of coming to live in England.' It was all so very sophisticated compared to the life he had been used to.

He told of going to Maurice Winnick's Mayfair offices and filling in the time waiting to see him by talking to the receptionist. She said she was getting married, to a seaman, and all the furniture for their flat had been bought.

'I've seen to it that it's in my name,' she said.

'Why's that?' asked Eamonn.

'Well, if anything goes wrong with the marriage at least I'll have the furniture.'

Eamonn said he was 'shocked' that anyone should enter a marriage with any thought that perhaps it might not last. When a good Irish Catholic got married, it was for ever.

He had to acquire his first dinner jacket and said that when he made his debut in front of the TV cameras he was wearing it without a tie. The occasion was his first boxing commentary for the BBC and since it was an evening transmission you of course went properly attired. However, when the fight was over and the producer got him to nip up into the ring for an interview with the victor his clip-on tie got caught on one of the ropes and the interview was conducted with Eamonn tieless. There was some question as to whether his new employers were as concerned about his appearing without a tie as they were about the fact that it had been a *clip-on* affair.

The BBC's attitude to such gaucheries was borne out some time after that when he was talking to Gilbert in the *What's My Line?* hospitality room and Gilbert remarked on the wedding ring he was wearing.

'You realise,' said Gilbert, 'that you have it on the wrong finger.'

'Third finger is correct, isn't it?'

'For women, yes,' said Gilbert, 'but men wear the wedding ring on the little finger. Do you know that if you were applying for a post in the Foreign Office and they noticed that, you would be rejected immediately.'

'It's as bad as that?'

'Dear boy, it is as bad as – as wearing a made-up bow tie.'

Since at the moment they were in dinner jackets, as always for *What's My Line?*, Eamonn said afterwards that he moved away before Gilbert took too close a look at the tie he had on. And he stopped wearing the wedding ring altogether.

When someone said to Gilbert that he felt sure that the rows on *What's My Line?* were staged, Gilbert's reply was: 'Oh no, they don't pay us enough to rehearse as well.'

Dicky Leeman, looking back on those twenty years, said to me: 'Of course there were rows, on and off the screen, but none of them any more spectacular that in any long running shows with people of different temperaments closely associated all the time.'

What in fact did Gilbert and Eamonn think of one another? Gilbert had a stock answer when asked how he felt about the show's chairman: 'I admire him professionally.'

When Gilbert died Eamonn was one of those who contributed to a book published in his memory – *By His Friends*. He wrote: 'at the back of Gilbert's irritability as a panellist was one important factor – the feeling he should be doing better, something that would make a greater demand on the talents he believed he had. Many of his more critical friends would tut-tut and pooh-pooh and say: "Really, dear chap, you should be dealing with higher things." These well-meaning people did him a disservice. They stimulated his already only too

74

ready to be stimulated unhappiness. They both over-estimated and under-estimated him. It was a situation I tried to remedy once. It was the last time we met privately before he died.'

The scene was a meal at the Caprice, a setting which Andrews did not feel was quite the place for a serious talk. However, he said that Gilbert, very depressed, spoke of being thoroughly frustrated at the BBC – they should send him around the world as an investigator extraordinary; he was doing nothing useful in his life.

Andrews told him he was not the intellectual he thought he was and that he should not get involved in 'brainstorming programmes' that were beyond him. He tried to explain to Gilbert that he was in 'a unique position for millions of viewers – a colossus astride the two camps'. He could let those who were not so intellectual know that eggheads were 'important but not impossible' and indicate to the eggheads that they had 'much to learn from those more interested in Floyd Patterson than Boris Pasternak'.

Gilbert, it seems, said: 'I never thought of it that way.'

Andrews concluded: 'I like to think that if he had gone on living he would have gone on thinking that way, that in time he would believe it.'

It is not recorded whether Harding had similarly done a detailed analysis of what was wrong with Eamonn Andrews. However, he did once say, 'Eamonn suffers from Irishness.'

CHAPTER 10

A HOME OF ONE'S OWN

Gilbert Harding's success with *What's My Line?* brought financial rewards which enabled him, among other things, to buy a delightful house in Brighton. He had come a long way from the Bradford workhouse.

His first home of his own – i.e., when not living-in at the numerous schools at which he taught and going back to live with mother between such jobs – had been a flat in Twickenham. It was shortly before the war and his choice of Twickenham was because his sister Connie was teaching at a school in the area. It was economical for them to share a flat and Gilbert was quite sentimental about 'the fun of installing furniture of one's own, collecting a few little treasures, and really feeling that once you had shut the front door behind you it was really home.' They moved into 11 Berkeley Court, London Road, Twickenham the day King Edward VIII abdicated, December 10, 1936.

Connie was a year older than he, 'but always much older in common sense'. As a young girl she was described by John Pollard, who grew up with the two of them, as 'a huge, giggling, good humoured lass, the sort of outrageous, rumbustious hoyden small boys admire', in contrast to 'her young brother, who was clever, difficult, remote, too grand for anyone'.

Vivien Barnsley, who went to school with Connie at the Hereford High School for Girls, recalls: She *was* a big girl, like her mother. Gilbert was big, too. They both inherited it from her. But I always used to envy Connie, She looked so good in the school uniform. You know what girl's uniforms are like. It *fitted* Connie. She had lovely blonde hair and beautiful skin and she was always so neat and tidy. It was a scruffy school and drab. She was in a form below me but I really was envious. She stood out from all the rest.'

Connie won a scholarship to the Teacher's Training College at Bingley in Yorkshire and from there went to the teaching post at the Hampton Wick County primary school in Twickenham. That was in the early 1930s when Gilbert, after a succession of dead-end jobs, had gone back to live with his mother in Bradford. He felt ashamed. 'The fact that Connie was settling into a worthwhile profession, self-contained, self-sufficient, and not in any way reliant on Mother, gave me some bad moments of conscience. "Where," I would ask myself, "are you heading? Was all Mother's effort to send you to Cambridge and equip you for a place in life going to amount to nothing?"'

By contrast, Connie at once became a particularly good teacher – 'the youngest ever to be appointed a headmistress in England,' friend Vivien recalls.

'Connie was terribly fond of Gilbert, or Gil, as she used to call him. Can you imagine anyone else calling him Gil? It would have been like calling Mortimer Wheeler – Mort. Anyway, I remember I was with her when Gilbert got his job with the BBC and how thrilled and excited she was about it. He liked her, too. But he was cruel to her in one respect. He stopped her from marrying a man she was in love with – a young Anglican clergyman. But Gilbert had become a Catholic, as you know. Gilbert talked to her about her Anglican minister. "You can't marry *him*," he said. "You can't marry a *heretic*." Connie never married.

'When Connie was getting older the neat and tidy look of her youth was no longer there. She rather let herself go and Gilbert felt that something should be done about her appearance. There was some sort of function coming up which all the people connected with *What's My Line?* were going to be at, so Gilbert took her to Bond Street and bought her a fabulous dress – a Dior or something; anyway no expense spared. At the party he drew Barbara Kelly aside and asked her: "How do you think Connie looks?" Barbara Kelly said: "She looks like an unmade bed." It broke his heart.

'Connie died very young, really. He was sad because she was still only in her forties.'

Mrs Harding lived with Gilbert and Connie in the Twickenham flat for a time, after she had retired from her work in Bradford, but early in the 1950s it was decided she should return to Hereford. Aunt Edie had become the last of the King family surviving there and Mrs Harding would go and live with her in a small but pleasant house owned by the Kings in one of the better parts of the town.

However, there was a snag. The house had been let furnished and the tenant and his family refused to move out. Gilbert had no option but to instruct the bailiffs to evict them – and learned of yet another of the hazards of fame. By then *What's My Line?* was in full swing and everything Gilbert did made news. He went to Vivien Barnsley's brother Paul, of the estate agents handling the property, and told him he was worried. He had received a letter from the tenant telling him that the *Daily Mirror* had been informed of the date of the eviction. In the event the *Mirror* did not follow up the tip-off, for reasons Gilbert never found out, and Mrs Harding and her sister were established in the house.

Mrs Vera Watson, a distant relative, used to take her young children from their home in Aldeburgh on the Suffolk coast to stay with Mrs Harding and Aunt Edie for the Easter holidays.

'It was so old inside the house,' she said, and epitomised the sort of place it was with the single phrase 'lace curtains and conches'. Many people will still remember conches – the large, trumpet-like shells which were regarded as attractive ornaments for the 'parlour' by the Victorians and others of a later era who lived in the past. It seemed a tendency of Aunt Edie to live in the past, for prominently displayed in a corner of the dining room was a basket weave wheelchair in which she and the other maiden aunt, Ethel, had given Grandfather King his outings during his declining years. The very look of it frightened the Watson children. They were not very taken, either, with Aunt Edie's high black button-up boots and her cats, which abounded. 'They thought she was a witch.' But nevertheless Mrs Watson, as she would sit sipping the bee wine Aunt Edie served, found her 'a sweet and gentle woman'.

After Connie had died Gilbert moved from Twickenham into London to a flat on the corner of Cadogan Place and Pont Street in Knightsbridge.

As secretary-companion he took on Roger Storey, a 27-year-old actor who had been working for a firm named Adprint while resting between engagements. 'Podge', as Gilbert was to call him, was to stay in the job until Gilbert died in 1960. He was one of only three beneficiaries in Gilbert's will.

Also living-in at the flat was Gilbert's driver or, rather, a succession of drivers. He had acquired a Ford Zephyr and having long ago decided – after hair-raising experiences in his ancient Jowett – that he was temperamentally unsuited to drive a motor car, it was necessary to hire a driver (not a chauffeur – he felt that term far too pretentious). He had to advertise numerous times for someone to fill the post, since in the ensuing years there was to be considerable turn-over in the job of Gilbert Harding's driver, for two main reasons.

First, there was not really a great deal of driving to do – most of it in the evening – going back and forth to broadcasts and hanging around waiting for Gilbert to emerge from a pub or other place from which he would make his unsteady way. So during most days the driver was expected to be a general factotum around the flat, which is not always to the taste of those in the chauffeur world. (It did, however, appeal to the first applicant, who had been a 'gentleman's gentleman' to a member of the nobility, which naturally impressed Gilbert. He was at once installed in the Cadogan Place *ménage*, but there was a flaw. The truth came out that he did not hold a driving licence and never had. 'No matter,' said Gilbert, reluctant to part with this tenuous link with the aristocracy. 'We shall see to it that you take lessons.' Nothing came of it).

The second reason was that it needs little imagination to envisage Gilbert as one of the worst back-seat drivers in England. He compounded it by invariably riding in the front seat. When in a puckish mood he liked to urge the driver, 'Faster! Faster!' Also he had a tendency when picked up after a heavy drinking session to fall asleep on his driver's shoulder. This more than once resulted in collisions, fortunately never serious.

Eventually Gilbert was lucky enough to find David Watkins, who was his reliable driver in the last years of his life and was in fact the only person closely connected with him who was with him when he died.

Mrs Harding came up from Hereford from time to time to stay for a while and when he was in his 'Regency buck' mood he would have liked to have taken her out for a drive around the park in an open carriage. Such things no longer being available, he did the next best thing – he would take her out in an open taxi.

There were still on the streets of London in the 1950s a type of cab which many people – but not the police – were sorry to see discontinued. Not hardtops like modern taxis, the back part had a collapsible hood which could be lowered on a pleasant day for passengers to drive along in the open air. When the hood was drawn it was cosy in there and secluded, since there was only one tiny, oval rear window. Courting couples in need of a taxi would let modern ones go by until they could hail one of these which had such delightful privacy in the back. The police called them 'brothel wagons' because prostitutes used them as a mobile substitute for their usual place of business, and they eventually had them taken off the road.

Gilbert, however, made full use of them in the summer when the hoods were down and he felt a delightful way to entertain his mother was to hail one and to say to the cabby: 'Would you be so good as to drive us to the Regent's Park.' He always called it *the* Regent's Park, as he felt sure those close to the Prince Regent must have done.

When Aunt Edie came up to London for a visit it was the way he showed her round the city. It was important that she see as much as possible, since this was her first visit to London for sixty years – an indication of the isolated life led by that maiden lady.

Handily placed around the corner from his flat, in Motcomb Street, was an excellent pub, 'The Turk's Head', which was to become well known for Gilbert's presence. It was on the corner of Kinnerton Street, where Hermione Gingold lived, and he was to add to his 'catalogue of crimes in the cause of what is called entertainment' by making his debut with her as a recording artist, singing *It Takes Two To Tango*. The record was banned by the BBC – not because of *Two To Tango* but because of what was on the other side. It was called *Oh, Grandma*! and was a send up of the Little Red Riding Hood story, with Gilbert as the wolf. What the BBC objected to were the lines:—Gilbert: 'Oh, Hermione, can I have you as a regular diet?' Hermione: 'Yes, Gilbert, but don't speak with your mouth full.' The joke was that the lyrics had had been written by Annette Mills, creator of *Muffin the Mule*, with a naive disregard for possible double meanings, as in the classic case of another Children's Hour contributor who did a piece for the kiddies called *Playing With Your Balls*, pirated recordings of which are now a collector's item.

Another favourite haunt of Gilbert's during his Cadogan Place period was 'The Queen's Elm' in Fulham Road. Sean Treacy, the landlord there, wrote in his book of reminiscences, *A Smell of Broken Glass:* 'Gilbert Harding could always command a bit of hush by his entrance. With his customary entourage – mostly male – he was like a dreadnought with its frail frigate escorts sailing into port.'

Sean Treacy expressed himself as 'frightened' of Gilbert's mother. Once when Gilbert was giving some sort of reception at which Mrs Harding was present, Treacy was invited and on arrival was offered a glass of champagne by Gilbert.

"I'm not a great champagne man," said the Irish publican. "I'd prefer to have a Guinness, if I may."

"Sorry, dear boy, we're all drinking champagne."

"But I *would* rather have a Guinness."

"Here you are," said Gilbert. "Champagne."

"Gillie," his mother snapped.

'Gilbert,' Treacy reports, 'jumped like a little boy caught with his hand in the biscuit jar.'

"If this gentleman wants a Guinness," Mrs Harding levelled at her 46-year-old-son, "he shall have a Guinness. Don't try to dictate to him what he should drink. Get him a Guinness, even if it means going out for it."

Meekly Gilbert took the tongue lashing. Treacy felt he would not like 'the plump, thin-lipped woman with jowls and a beaky nose' to turn on him. He sensed that when roused she would be vicious.

Just how much so we shall come to see, when one accusation in particular she hurled at Gilbert was so vicious as to have an effect on him so profound that it destroyed him, removed from him any pleasure he had left in life.

While he was at Cadogan Place, Gilbert was approached by Fielden Hughes, who ran a radio programme called *Say the Word*, on which he wanted him to appear. Harding asked him to come round to the flat to discuss it. On arrival Hughes, a former headmaster of Willesden County Secondary School, was rather taken aback when Gilbert said to him: 'I am about to take a bath. Come in with me and sit on the loo and tell me all about your show.' Hughes thought it was somewhat irregular but shrugged it off on the basis that he was dealing with Gilbert Harding the eccentric. ('In the bath he looked like a floundering porpoise.')

Through the fumes of 'sickly bath essence' Hughes told him that it was a travelling show on the Light Programme, playing a different town each week and pitting three locals against a word expert. Gilbert was to make regular appearances on *Say the Word* and thoroughly enjoyed the proceedings, especially one programme in which the Chairman of the Brighton Education Committee when asked 'If an aviary is a place for birds, what is an apiary?' answered 'A place for apes.'

He and Fielden Hughes got on very well, primarily because they shared a common background of schoolteaching. Also Gilbert was impressed by the fact that Hughes was, then not now, father-in-law of Mai Zetterling. Hughes admired him as an epicure. 'Gilbert quite agreed with Arnold Bennett – "The best is good enough for me."' Hughes recalls being in the snack bar of a pub with Gilbert before a broadcast and his ordering a plate of smoked salmon for each of them. When it came it was seen to be cut to the thinness often encountered in such places. With a fork Gilbert disdainfully lifted a piece of the salmon and said to the man in the chef's cap behind the counter: 'You almost missed.' Hughes enjoyed Harding's neat turn of phrase. Once when their travels took them to Hereford, Gilbert took Hughes to his old haunt, 'The Green Dragon', and while they were there they became aware of a young man who was making rather a fool of himself at the bar. Harding knew him as the scion of one of the well-to-do families in the area and he said to Hughes: 'Oh, don't mind him. He has a private income. He's an income poop.'

It was also Hughes who was to try to get Gilbert to be less impatient with autograph-hunters and other fans – 'They are your customers, you cannot do without them' – and as we shall see shortly Gilbert took him into his confidence about his homosexuality and the efforts he made to free himself of it.

Gilbert Harding was often misjudged as far as rudeness and outlandish behaviour were concerned. In 1954 when his mother was gravely ill in a nursing home in Hereford and he went down to be with her, the townspeople were critical of him for being callously indifferent. One day when news got around that Mrs Harding was nearing the end they were shocked that he had been seen in the town and was not at her bedside. They became even more appalled when it was learned that he had gone to the cinema.

Mrs Drucilla Pederson recalls that day very clearly. She was at the Ritz Cinema that afternoon when Gilbert came in and sat down just a few seats away. 'He never looked at the screen,' she told me. 'I'm sure he had no idea what film it was. He just sat there, in tears.'

He *had* been at the nursing home. His mother was dead.

How deeply this affected him was revealed to the general public six years later in an interview with John Freeman which became one of the most widely discussed broadcasts ever presented on British television.

Meanwhile for Gilbert there were the prosaic things to settle up in Hereford. It was decided that Aunt Edie, being alone now, should move into a home where she could be looked after properly and Gilbert had to make arrangements for the selling of the house. Paul Barnsley of the estate agents told me: 'One man who was interested made an offer which was below my valuation but because he was blind I thought I should submit the offer to Gilbert with appropriate remarks. He instructed me at once to sell at the price the man had offered and the sale went through accordingly.'

That year, 1954, Harding moved into a flat in a fashionable block in Weymouth Street, within walking distance of Broadcasting House and *ipso facto*, such drinking venues as the BBC club, the ML (Marie Lloyd) club and the surrounding pubs frequented by the broadcasters and inevitably called 'the BBC pubs'. Handiest for Gilbert was 'The Devonshire Arms,' also regularly used by a veteran radioman from the North who, although famous on his programme for giving money away, had 'paralysed arms' when it came to buying a round. Gilbert once said of him: 'He's so stingy he has his toothbrushes rebristled.'

For such Hardingisms he was to become a legend in and around Broadcasting House; his reputation as wit, eccentric and master of the insult spread far afield as people dined out on their favourite 'Gilbert Harding stories'.

Ian Messiter remembers being with Harding in one of the BBC pubs when a television performer of no great talent was bemoaning his lack of work. 'It is very sad, isn't it,' said Harding. 'Some people think they are being ignored when they are merely forgotten.'

On another occasion much toasting was being done of a pair who were about to be married and a then magazine editor said, 'They'll make a very happy couple.' 'You should know,' said Gilbert, 'you've slept with both of them.'

One evening in the ML club, last stopping-off place for Harding on his way home since it was open after the pubs shut, there was a man prominent in the newspaper world of the 1950s who suffered from clicking dentures, which disturbed Gilbert and his friends in view of the fact that it was very much noticed during his radio and TV appearances. 'He really must do something about them' was the feeling of the group when he was nearby, whereupon Gilbert, with his voice at its most resounding, said: 'False teeth are like children. They should be seen and not heard.' (It was to no avail. The man still clicks away on radio and television.)

Once Harding was chatting with colleagues over drinks in the BBC club when they were joined by a tedious member of the executive staff who proceeded boringly to take over what had hitherto been a pleasant session. 'I'll tell you something,' Harding said to him. 'When I leave the BBC I am going to go around in turn to each person in the Corporation whom I have found odious and tell them exactly what I think of them. But in your case I can't wait. Fuck off.'

It was Harding who gave the nickname to the spire of All Souls Church, directly opposite the entrance to Broadcasting House. It is a conical spire, rising to a sharp point, and one day coming out of Broadcasting House with a friend he glanced up at it and said: 'The parachutist's nightmare.'

But undoubtedly Gilbert's most famous 'in joke' as far as Broadcasting House was concerned, was when he was in one of the studios about to do a broadcast and he took a drink from the glass of water to clear his throat. He gave an agonised look. Clearly the water was not fresh. He called in one of the studio assistants and pointed to the offending article. 'Kindly replace this immediately.' he said. 'Surely you know better than to give me the glass of water Lord Reith kept his false teeth in.'

Gilbert's flat at 6 Weymouth Court, now occupied by a doctor since it is handy also to Harley Street, is in a building that was put up in 1910, when purpose-built blocks of flats were a relatively new idea. The term 'flat' derives from the fact that it used to have the meaning of a storey and the original flats were the usual rooms of a house condensed on to one floor of a building. Which was precisely what Gilbert's flat looked like – six rooms besides the kitchen and bathroom. Off the long, L-shaped corridor was a study for Podge, his secretary, the master bedroom for Gilbert, two other bedrooms, living room and dining room. Brian Masters, a later friend, said that apart from some pieces which

Gilbert had brought up from his mother's Hereford home, 'it was furnished like a men's club – big comfortable chairs you could sink into.'

There was little to be seen of pictures on the wall and suchlike, with one exception . . . Gilbert had met Marlene Dietrich by virtue of being asked to introduce her act at the Café de Paris. He got on extremely well with 'the beautiful and desirable Marlene' and when she arrived in London in the following year he was the first person she contacted. He had sent to the airport, 'to await arrival', one of his gigantic 'flower power' gestures and she wanted to thank him. They happily renewed their close relationship.

In direct contrast to the home of his mother's family in Hereford, which had family portraits the way other people have mice, there was only one solitary framed photograph in the Weymouth Court flat of Gilbert. It was a picture, affectionately inscribed, of Marlene.

The masculinity of the furnishings was appropriate to Gilbert's male-orientated group of intimate friends. Vivien Barnsley said: 'My brother Paul and I didn't see much of Gilbert after he became famous and rich. One time when Paul came up from Hereford he went to look Gilbert up. Paul got involved in some sort of party that was going on in the flat and when eventually he came back to my place he looked downcast. I asked him what the trouble was and he said, "Gilbert has some funny friends now."

Brian Masters is an author. He has done ten books by the present count and the subjects include Camus, Sartre and Marie Corelli. He is of medium height and slight build, neatly turned out. He is good-looking. He was 37 when I met him but looked younger. He is well spoken, which I was to learn had much to do with Gilbert Harding. He told me how his friendship with Gilbert began.

In 1957 when he was at school at Wilson's Grammar in Camberwell, he and some of the other boys decided that the school should have a magazine and to ensure the largest possible circulation it was felt that it should appeal to the staff as well as the pupils. Young Brian thought that the way to do this would be to carry in each issue an interview with a famous person. And for the first interview why not start at the top with the most famous man in England – Gilbert Harding.

He wrote to Harding and a couple of days later was summoned to the headmaster's study; there was a phone call for him. Harding said, 'Come to tea on Tuesday, four o'clock.'

The young grammar school boy rang the bell at 6 Weymouth Court at the appointed time and was ushered in by Roger Storey. He was told that Mr Harding was on the phone, did he mind waiting? It was hardly necessary to tell him the subject of his interview was on the phone since as he stood there holding his school cap, trembling, he could hear the voice booming out from the living room – in violent altercation, as it often tended to be during a telephone call.

After a wait of an hour of increasing nerves the call was finished and the intrepid cub-reporter was taken into the big room, where Harding was seated in pyjamas and dressing gown at a table surrounded by what seemed to be, in rememberance, six telephones. It was, anyway, an impressive array and Harding ceremoniously took the receiver off each of them as the boy came in. To put him at his ease Harding asked him whether he would like to hear a joke he had just heard, which turned out to be one of which Podge disapproved but Harding said to him for heaven's sake the lad was clearly old enough now to appreciate such a joke.

He was then at his most helpful to the interviewer of the *Wilson's Grammar School Gazette* for the next two hours, after which he announced: 'I shall now have a bath and then, young Brian, I'll take you out to dinner.'

It is not given to many Cockney schoolboys to have their evening meal at Grosvenor House. From Camberwell to Park Lane for dinner – young Masters was wide-eyed as he and his 50-year-old host were escorted across the spacious, high-ceilinged dining room of the hotel to 'a table for Mr Harding'.

But it was then that the boy, who had been in some sort of seventh heaven at all the time the great man had devoted to him and his thoughtfulness towards him, saw for the first time the other side of Gilbert Harding. 'It was as though, right on cue, now that he was out among other people, he changed to his public image, what they expected of him. From being a kindly, gentle man with me in the flat he became aggressive, rude to the waiters, argumentative. I was acutely embarrassed, being at the focal point of it all there with him as everybody looked round at our table.'

That meeting with Gilbert Harding was the start of a close association between the man in his fifties and the boy in his teens which went on until Harding died. 'He took me in hand,' Masters will tell you. 'I was just a Cockney lad. My accent was pure Camberwell. Gilbert spoke the best English I have ever heard. He would constantly correct me – in private, in a kindly way, never in front of anybody. Never say "pleased to meet you", he would say, or "ever so", or "indoors" when you mean "at home". You're a bright boy, he would say to me, but it isn't bright to use long words when there are perfectly good short ones you can use instead. He was doing a Pygmalion with me. I was his Eliza Dolittle.'

In due course Masters won a scholarship to university and since his parents had moved to Cardiff he chose University College there. Harding by then was living mainly in Brighton, coming up to London only when he was required for a radio or TV programme, and he gave Masters free run of the Weymouth Street flat, to live there when he was not attending college.

It was an arrangement that was to the advantage of Roger Storey, for he could be spared from the permanent watch over Gilbert. By that time of his life the state of his health was such that he could never be left alone. The machine brought into action when he had a severe asthma attack was bulky, about the size of a small kitchen refrigerator, and it was not possible for him to operate it himself when he was in the throes of an attack. With young Brian on hand, his secretary could get out and about for a change. At the shout of 'Boy!' from some part of the extensive flat, Brian would rush to wherever Harding was and revive him with the machine. More than once it was a close call. On one occasion Brian reached Harding to find him motionless on the floor, his face a ghastly colour. He thought he was dead.

On Sunday nights when Harding would come home at midnight or thereabouts following an unwinding session after *What's My Line?* he would take Brian into his favourite part of the flat, the kitchen, there to mount his stool and with a drink and inevitable cigarette in one hand and, the other hand free to attend to the supper he was cooking, he would chat with his protégé, or, rather, conduct a monologue. 'I didn't mind that Gilbert did all the talking, because I was learning all the time.' It was not uncommon for these kitchen interludes to go on until 4 a.m. by which time Gilbert had had so much to drink that he was likely to collapse on the floor in mid-sentence. 'And I would have to drag him – all seventeen stone of him – to bed.'

Brian Masters remembers what he feels was the worst *faux pas* he has ever made. 'Although I was then just a Cockney lad, Gilbert never excluded me from the company when people came. I was often embarrassed and inevitably out of my depth, but Gilbert felt it was part of my education. Peter Daubeny, the theatrical impresario, came to discuss some project with Gilbert and before he arrived Gilbert warned me that he had lost one arm and the empty sleeve which hung at his side was something about which he was self-conscious.

'I sat there like a bump on a log as they talked. But I remembered something Gilbert had told me about G. K. Chesterton, whom he had known well. Chesterton had said: "There are no uninteresting people, only uninterested people." So I felt I should make some sort of contribution and when there was a lull in their conversation I piped up, "What have you got up your sleeve for your next production, Mr Daubeny?"

'It was a ghastly moment but Gilbert rushed in to save my face and afterwards he was so kind and understanding about it.

'But sometimes he was abominable to me. I remember once he had me in tears and as I was standing against the mantlepiece crying, Hector Bolitho came and put his arm around me and comforted me.

'Gilbert was a pederast. He liked young men, but it was on a high plane. He was a man of class. There was nothing sordid about it. He used to like to come in when I was having a bath and sit and chat with me and then when I was out of the bath he would dry me down with the towel.'

The young 'Cockney lad' went on from Cardiff to Montpellier University in the South of France and graduated with first class honours. But there was a hollow ring to his sense of achievement. 'Gilbert would have been so pleased. In fact I had been determined to do well as much for him as for myself. But he died several months previously. It would have made him so happy to have known before he died. I wasn't even there with him at the end. None of the people close to him were. I was in Montpellier and had no warning to dash over and be with him.

'I'll always regret that my results came through too late, for him. He had told me so many times – it was really the basis of our whole friendship – that I was the one who was going to avoid the mistakes he had made in his own life. And an important one was that he felt he had wasted his time at university.'

The move to Brighton, with the London flat still retained, was made in 1956. The house cost Gilbert £4,000 and he spent as much on improvements; at today's values it would be worth at least ten times his purchase price. It is at No. 20 Montpelier Villas, a street on the ridge running up from the sea front in the centre of town, and is one of the cluster of attractive three-storey semi-detached houses each with its own small, neat garden. It is of white stucco, relieved by black-painted iron grillwork; early Victorian and therefore the simple, gracious lines of the Regency period are still in evidence, the only indication of Victorian ornamentation being in the balcony with the canopy above which runs around the front of the huge bay window dominating the facade.

Gilbert was one of the large contingent of well known entertainment personalities and writers who set up a colony, in Brighton in the 1950s which is still very much a feature of the town. Laurence Olivier, John Clements, . . . Douglas Byng, famous pantomime dame of between the wars . . . song-writer David Henniker, John Montgomery, the author, Alan Melville, playwright and master of the revue sketch . . . Elizabeth Allan, Dora Bryan and Millicent Martin . . . the late John Watt, BBC producer, Hector Bolitho, and others.

One of the great attractions for these London-based celebrities was that they could live by the sea and take advantage of one of the best railway commuter services in the world. They could be at their theatre, broadcasting studios or publishers in London, fifty miles away, in an hour, travelling in the unashamed luxury of the old 'Brighton Belle'.

In Pears Cyclopaedia, the listing for Brighton gives the terse details of location and population, and site of Royal Pavilion and university, and then as the only other solitary fact about Brighton chosen to pass on to its readers: 'Birthplace of Aubrey Beardsley'. This was either an arbitrary choice or an intended backhander at the other large colony there of those without his talent but who share his inclinations.

The late Hector Bolitho was a neighbour of Gilbert's in Brighton and his success as a writer about Royalty was due in no small measure to the fact that he was very friendly with the then Dean of Windsor, who allowed him unlimited use of the archives there. He was effeminate and was referred to on numerous occasions, even in print, as Hector Blithero. He was a figure of fun to more than a few people. Alan Melville told me of one time being with Gilbert out on the little balcony which skirted the bay window at the front of his house. They were discussing Bolitho, and Gilbert had no sooner said, 'That man and all those bloody books of his on Royalty', when there he was coming down the road. He looked up at them sheepishly. Had he heard? It did not seem to deter Gilbert. 'Hullo, Hector,' his voice boomed out. 'How's Queen Victoria?'

Alan Melville lived just two streets away from Gilbert, in the house he still occupies. He recalls that 'so many times Gilbert would say to me that he was just wasting his life, he had never achieved anything. And I'd have to say to him, "Good gracious, Gilbert, that face of yours only needs to appear on the box and at once you hold the whole nation in the palm of your hand. How can you say you have never achieved anything?"

' "Oh no, dear boy, I don't mean that," he would say. "What I mean is that I've never *created* anything. I envy you so. You're writing your plays and radio and television programmes, you're creating something all the time. That's achievement."

'I would have to tell him that I was the one who envied *him*. He had none of the hard grind of churning out a script, rehearsals, learning lines and all that back-breaking, nerve-wracking work. What an achievement to be able to go on television and just be himself.'

Melville said he never cured Gilbert of this sense of non-achievement but he was at length able to get across to him the basic difference in way of life between the creative television man which he, Melville, was and the pure and simple 'TV personality' which was Gilbert's fortunate rôle.

Between programmes and personal appearances Gilbert really had nothing to do. So, why not drop around to see his good friend Alan – invariably for 'liquid elevenses'? Early in their friendship Melville would break off from his typewriter because he realised that Gilbert did not understand that just because a person is at home it does not mean he is not working and, after all, they were enjoyable chats. 'However,' Melville told me, 'I came to dread the sound of my front gate being opened and that famous voice intoning: "Where is that alleged star of stage, screen and radio?" Things got so bad, my work being interrupted so much, that I had to take to hiding in the boot cupboard. Eventually, though, I was able to get Gilbert to see that it was a hard slog for us, if not for such as he, and he only came around when he knew I was free.'

Besides his secretary and his driver, Gilbert had a third person living in the house. Joan Smith had been a buyer with one of the big stores in Bradford and had met Gilbert through knowing his mother.

She was a cut above being merely a paid housekeeper. Mrs Embery – 'Midge' – the traditional English 'treasure' (inherited by Alan Melville when Gilbert died) came in to do the daily chores and Joan Smith performed the function of being companion to Gilbert. He would take her on what he called 'treats' to the Theatre Royal in Brighton, where many of the big shows bound for the West End would be tried out. People invited to a party given by Gilbert would wonder by what circuitous route an entertainment star such as Pearl Bailey was to be found sharing a drink with him on the patio of his house – and then realise she was at the theatre in transit to London.

Joan Smith was to learn that although the much discussed scenes Gilbert created were usually at a pub or a restaurant, another venue for Harding eccentricities was the theatre. He had the tendency to go to sleep at the play, which his companion invariably knew was to be expected and the prodding of Gilbert to wake him up was resorted to only when he started to snore. His attention could be held, though, by a really bad play and he enjoyed doing a running commentary on its awfulness.

When Henry Kendall arrived in Brighton with an offering called *On Monday Next* for a try-out prior to going to the West End, not only was the show a disaster but one of the actors was particularly inept. When he came to the line 'I've been offered a part in Manchester Rep' – 'Take it!' the voice of Harding echoed through the theatre.

Bill Thomson was his companion at the opening of Noel Coward's *Quadrille* and when they were among those invited backstage afterwards it was the first time Gilbert met the Master. Bill Thompson reports: 'As they were introduced, Noel said "Gilbert Harding!" with a fine display of being impressed. He then kissed him on the cheek, which rather took Gilbert aback.

"And what did you think of my show?" Noel asked.

"I'm afraid I slept right through it," Gilbert felt prompted to say.

"Don't worry about that, dear fellow," said Noel. "I've slept through *so* many of yours."

Joan Smith told a friend that in view of the fact that she professed to being no great cook, Gilbert delighted in preparing meals for the two of them. 'He would get things started in the kitchen before he settled down to the evening's TV viewing. He was an absolute addict. So much so that he would sit himself down in a chair in the doorway of the living room so that he could watch the BBC on the set in that room and at the same time see ITV on the other set in the dining room. Then he slipped out to the kitchen to do this or that to whatever he was making when there was a dull patch or during the adverts. The result was that getting the meal organised took a long time. I'd sit there getting hungrier and hungrier, but the food wasn't on the table until midnight, when television had shut down.'

He talked so much, with affection, about his housekeeper-companion that she became known as 'Gilbert's Miss Smith'. At a party an intoxicated lady was introduced to 'Gilbert's Miss Smith' and came away muttering, 'Who'd ever have guessed it?'

'Who'd ever have guessed what?' someone asked the sozzled female.

'Who'd ever guess that Gilbert Harding hops into bed with *her*?'

'What on earth are you talking about?'

'Well, I've just met her and the chap who introduced us said "This is Gilbert's mistress." '

One August Bank holiday when Podge and Gilbert's current driver were away visiting their families, he and Joan Smith were alone together over the long weekend. Neighbours, ever on the *qui vive* for juicy titbits about Gilbert to relay to friends, nodded their heads knowingly. Melville, no mere gossiping neighbour, said: 'She was in love with him. She would have liked nothing better than for him to have married her.'

When Gilbert died he left Joan Smith not a penny in cash – but something more worthwhile . . . Harding's solicitor was David Jacobs who represented many prominent show biz personalities, including Zsa Zsa Gabor, to name but a handful. He drew up Gilbert's will in September 1959 and when it was read in the following year it was revealed that there were only three beneficiaries. Aunt Edith King received an annuity of £250. She was the only surviving member of the Harding and King families whose lives had revolved around the Union Workhouse in Hereford. So as far as the family was concerned there was only this token gesture towards his 80-year-old aunt. To whom, then, did he leave the bulk of his estate?

It seemed a measure of his loneliness that sadly – for a man at the height of his fame, 'the most famous man in Britain' – when he was drawing up his will it was, it appears, a matter of asking himself who was around at the time – oh yes, his housekeeper and his secretary. To Joan Smith – his single important property holding, his home in Brighton, with provision made that funds should be made available from his estate to secure the freehold for her. To Roger Storey – the remainder of his estate.

How much did he leave? Today £27,615 may not seem any fortune, but in 1960 it was a tidy sum.

Not unnaturally Gilbert became one of Brighton's best known personalities.

John Montgomery, the author who still lives there, knew him well, having previously had close contact with him when he was on the staff of A. D. Peters, the literary agents who handled the books that went out under Gilbert's name. He told me of coming upon him outside a pub called 'The Colonnade' in New Road, Brighton, after closing time one afternoon. Gilbert was sprawled across the bonnet of a taxi and the driver was trying to persuade him to get into the cab. The pub was next door to the Theatre Royal, where a long queue at the booking office watched with interest the efforts of the cabby to help the country's most famous television star around to the open door of the taxi.

Montgomery joined in with a plea to Gilbert to let the two of them help him but he remained wedded to the bonnet of the cab. A policeman arrived and enquired what was going on.

'Nothing much, constable,' said Montgomery. 'We're getting him into the taxi. He's not feeling very well.'

Gilbert turned to look at the policeman and then slowly raised himself upright and stood, unsupported, swaying slightly.

'Constable Brown,' he said, 'my dear Constable Brown. How very nice to see you. How are you, my dear fellow. And how is your charming wife, and your little girl . . . Janet?'

Constable Brown beamed. 'They're both very well thank you, Mr Harding.'

'You must remember to give them my kind regards. I see them in church, you know, but there isn't always an opportunity to talk to them. You must give them my best wishes. But don't say you've seen me the worse for wear. I wouldn't like – well, *you know*, my dear fellow, they might not understand.'

'I won't say anything, Mr Harding. And now, how about getting into the taxi and then you can go home.'

'Quite right, my dear sir, you're absolutely right.'

Gilbert allowed himself to be helped in and through the open window, said: 'The good Miss Smith has my luncheon all ready for one o'clock.'

'And it's now after half past two,' Montgomery said. 'So you go straight home. No clubs, Gilbert. Straight home.'

'Clubs? My dear boy, whatever do you take me for? Off we go, then. And don't forget to remember me to your charming family, constable. Good afternoon.'

And as the taxi turned the corner into North Street a large white hand fluttered at a window. It was Gilbert saying goodbye – to his audience, the box-office queue?

John Montgomery said that when Gilbert died all the London papers sent reporters down here to dig up some scandal about him.

'They went around the town, especially in the pubs, asking, "Did he come in here and pick up boys?" and "Did he behave very badly in here?" But they found no one willing to say anything against Gilbert – not even for money. That's how fond people were of him and how loyal they were to him. A taxi driver told me that one newspaper reporter asked him if he had ever driven Gilbert home.

' "Oh, yes, frequently."

' "Very drunk, was he?"

' "Sometimes he'd had a few. Like you reporters do."

' "And did he take boys home with him in the cab?"

' "Good lord, no, he never did anything like that. He didn't have to. He had thousands of friends. Everyone liked him. He was very generous, and every Christmas he used to send my wife a Christmas card. He'd never ever met her, but he'd asked me for her address. He paid for one of our drivers to go with his wife and family on holiday in Jersey. He was always helping people. There aren't many like him around. He was a real gentleman." '

The Fleet Street reporters could search in vain for evidence of Gilbert picking up young men in Brighton. Because he was too discreet to do so on his own doorstep? That would seem to have been the explanation. But Montgomery gave me the real reason: 'He didn't need to. He had plenty of young friends locally he could entertain in his own home.'

CHAPTER II

TO COPE WITH FAME

Television gave rise to an entirely new type of fame. Like the new sort of coffee that came into wide use at the same time as the TV explosion, it was instant fame. Television was capable of making people famous *literally* overnight.

Previously the cliché 'famous overnight' had in truth meant success that invariably had been hard won. An actor, boxer, author or whatever had spent years learning his trade in obscurity before suddenly and excitingly recognition was achieved. Such is the impact of television, however, that fame can be achieved without the necessity of all those years of spadework, perfecting your craft. You gain instant fame just by *appearing*.

In the 1950s an actor named Robert Morley made his first appearance on *What's My Line?* and was a big hit. In a press interview afterwards he was asked about future TV appearances. 'There won't be any,' he said. 'Television is all wrong. You can be on the stage for thirty years working diligently at your craft and be hardly known by the general public; you appear for thirty minutes on some quiz show on television and overnight you are a nationally known figure, people stop you in the street. It is all too easy, the values are all wrong.'

Morley was intelligent enough to recognise the artificiality of television fame. Similarly, Marghanita Laski, writing of her appearances on *What's My Line?*: 'I suffered acute feelings of guilt of achieving fame, recognition and numerous social perks as reward for ability to play a simple parlour game. I got out because I was frightened.' Both Morley and Miss Laski were sufficiently well-adjusted to go back on their word and return to *enjoy* the financial and other rewards of being on television. Gilbert Harding was not so well-adjusted. J.B. Priestley wrote of him: 'Television suffers from a false importance. It can make reputations very quickly but they are not solid reputations, they are easy-come easy-go. One reason poor Gilbert Harding was so unhappy was that he knew he was perched on a vast, rotten mushroom.' *The Times* made the comment: 'Numerous programmes thrust him into a prominence which only a handful of people of exceptional talent could enjoy – or endure. The psychological strain of his sudden massive success produced in him a mental distress, which manifested itself by an extreme irritability and emotional disturbance.'

Robin Day, in his book *Television: A Personal Report*, wrote: 'The lives of famous TV figures may have been transformed by constant recognition and publicity, as in the case of Gilbert Harding, who became the prisoner of his television image.'

It would seem that of the hazards of being famous through television the most difficult to cope with is the constant recognition mentioned by Robin Day. In 1958 in one of his columns for the *People*, Harding wrote: 'You can go nowhere without being talked to – or rather, talked at. "You don't know me but I know you" is the sickening opening gambit for hundreds of these tedious conversations.'

Recognition by the general public is inescapable. I recall one time in a pub the name of Eamonn Andrews being mentioned and a Cockney sparrow piped up: 'I once met Eamonn Andrews, didn't I ?'

'Did you ?'

'Yeah. At London Airport. I'd had a few beers. I was having a slash, wasn't I ? And he came in and stood beside me. And I said, "You're Eamonn Andrews, aren't you ?" And he said "yes" and I said, "Where are you going ?" And he said: "I'm going to Ireland for a holiday." And I said: "That's nice for you." And he put his away and I put mine away and we went out.'

Robin Day's first taste of what he felt was a ridiculous situation as regards TV fame came early in his TV career when he went to cover a Tory Conference for ITN. He was taken aback when delegates swarmed around him asking for his autograph, when eminent politicians such as the Prime Minister, the Chancellor of the Exchequer and the Home Secretary were standing nearby. Unlike Harding, however, he learned to look at it objectively. Very sensibly he enjoys to the full the perks that come the way of a 'TV face'. Service in restaurants and hotels, at airports and so on is that extra bit better, people go out of their way to help and things are arranged more quickly. 'Handiest of all, cheques can be cashed in all sorts of places without any difficulty.' To his way of thinking 'these things make up for the irritations of being recognised on holiday and having to think up a new and if possible polite answer to the eternal "You don't know me but I know you." '

He might have taken his cue from Noel Coward, who had just one answer, effective and typically Coward. When a stranger started off 'You don't know me – 'he would interject: 'Oh, but I do. How's Mabel ?'

Coward was indeed the Master when it came to coping with this situation, even when the person accosting him might himself have a measure of fame. A movie actor much featured in virile roles once approached him and said: 'I'm Burt Reynolds.' 'Of course you are, dear chap,' said Noel. 'Of course you are.'

Michael Barrett confirms Robin Day's feeling that holidays are the worst time. 'You dare not go to Majorca or the South of Spain because all the English people there on holiday have the spare time to single you out for a nice long chat. You find yourself looking through the travel folders to find places unpopular with British tourists.'

David Nixon tells of being on holiday in Athens and going up to the Acropolis. Seeing the Parthenon was something he had long been looking forward to and so that his visit would not be spoiled he went early in the morning to avoid the coachloads of tourists. In solitude he stood there entranced. 'I was overwhelmed,' he told me. 'To be actually standing there among the columns of the Temple of Athena, built by Pericles two thousand years ago. Then some perky Cockney came out from behind a pillar and said, "Ullo, Davie-boy. What brings you 'ere? 'Avin' a n'oliday?" '

Nixon said that becoming a 'TV face' means that you have to change completely your life style. He dare not go into a strange pub. He goes only to the one where he is known, his local in the out-of-the-way part of Surrey where he lives. He never does any shopping, has to have it done for him. He knows that if he does go into a shop people will come up to him and say, 'Surely you don't have to *buy* those things. Surely you can make them materialise out of thin air.' When he pulls up at traffic lights, he *knows* that the motorist who stops beside him is going to call out: 'Come on, David, how about making all this traffic disappear?'

'I always join in their laughter, because they think those quips are something they have just invented. And the number of times I've heard those gags is now in the thousands.'

Gilbert, of course, made no attempt to change his way of life to fit in with his TV fame. He remained a pub lover throughout and the idea of finding an out-of-the-way pub to concentrate on would have been to court boredom. Also, unlike Nixon, he was never able fully to keep in check his natural inclination not to suffer fools gladly.

He gave short shrift to strangers who hurled at him either of the two unsolicited remarks which came *his* way with tedious monotony – 'What's *my* line, Gilbert?' and 'How's your indigestion?', the latter being prompted by his commercials for Macleans stomach powders.

Tom Sloan said of him: 'He was a wonderful friend and a kind man whose public image was his private misfortune.'

He was impatient with intruders on his private life. When Michael

Noakes was painting his portrait, which was to hang in the Royal Academy, they took a break from one of the sittings to go for a meal at one of the big Brighton hotels. In the washroom beforehand a man came up to Gilbert and said: 'You don't know who I am, do you?' Gilbert said no. The man told him his name and grasping Gilbert by the hand he started pumping it vigorously. 'I'm a dentist and I'm going to be on *What's My Line?* in a couple of weeks. And do you know what I'm going to say?' 'No,' said Gilbert, trying to free himself, 'I do not know what you are going to say.' 'I'm going to say I lead a hand-to-mouth existence. Ha, ha, ha!' As the loud laughter echoed around the porcelain Gilbert extracted his hand, and hurried unsmilingly out of the place. The dentist's laughter died abruptly and he looked hurt and bewildered.

Dicky Leeman once went with him to London's Marylebone Station to get a train to Leicester to visit Isobel Barnett and they made the mistake of not realising that special trains go from there to Wembley on big match days. They found the station jampacked with Leeds Rugby League fans down for their Cup Final. At one of the tea stalls they managed to get cups of tea to fill in the waiting time, when a voice echoed across the station: 'Eeeee! It's Gilbert 'Arding!' He and Leeman were engulfed in rattle-waving, rosetted League fans. Gilbert raised himself to his full height and boomed: 'My friend and I are endeavouring to have a quiet cup of tea before our departure for Leicester. Kindly go away and leave us alone.'

Oddly enough, one of the hazards of Gilbert's special sort of fame which he had to endure he had in common with Jack Dempsey. When Dempsey retired from the ring he became a restaurateur and it was not long before he had to be constantly on his guard when standing at his bar talking to customers. He had to watch out for someone coming up to him and, without any warning, throwing a punch at him. 'Object of the operation,' Dempsey said, 'was for the guy to be able to tell everyone for the rest of his life, "I'm the man who knocked out the great Jack Dempsey." '

In Harding's case it was not physical. In the pubs he liked to frequent he would be chatting with another customer when suddenly someone would approach him and without any preamble start to sound off with insulting remarks at him. 'It gets so monotonously tiresome,' he once said, 'strangers coming up to me and being as rude as they possibly can, just so that they can go home to their wives, boast to their friends, "I certainly put Gilbert Harding in his place." '

On occasion it did become physical. Jack House told me that on one occasion when he was doing his 'entertaining Gilbert after the show bit' they wound up in a pub in the Glasgow dock area. Shipyard workers who had just come off shift poured into the pub. As they got down to their drinking one of them caught sight of Harding and at once went over to him and began assailing him verbally. Harding made a comment to the effect that he did not feel like having 'a battle of wits with an unarmed adversary'. That, to a Glaswegian shipyard worker, called for only one course of action. Jack House needed the help of the burly landlord before they were able to get him away from the punch-up and into the street.

At another time Harding was in a pub in Tiger Bay, not the most salubrious part of Cardiff but a rendezvous for visiting broadcasters because despite the sleazy atmosphere of the bar it had a restaurant which, strangely, served French food of the highest quality. Among those at the bar was a woman who had had rather too much to drink. The sight of Harding obviously brought to her mind something he had said in an edition of *We Beg To Differ*. He had asked Gladys Young what she thought was the ideal holiday and when she replied, 'One spent in the mountains of Wales', he said: 'But how do you get away from the people?' The outcry that created even went to the extent of an official protest to the BBC from the Welsh Tourist Board.

In the Tiger Bay bar this clearly rankled with the Welsh woman in her cups, for with no other introductory remark than something on the lines of 'So you don't like the Welsh!' she broke the top of her glass on the edge of the bar and with the jagged remainder made for Harding. Blood was spilt but, with other customers restraining her, fortunately for Gilbert is was not very much.

Other women were more friendly towards him. It may have seemed odd but he had sex appeal for more than a few of them. Those of us who knew him and anyone seeing photographs of him now would wonder how he could possibly excite a woman. No Errol Flynn he, as *Time* would have put it in those days when they used such laboured inversions. He was overweight. He wore glasses not quite of the tonic-bottle-bottom type as those worn by the late Lord Thomson but of a sort that obtrusively branded him as bespectacled. He had a military moustache which would have looked jaunty on a dashing major but did nothing at all for him. His general appearance had something in common with such as Malcolm Muggeridge and Sir Alec Douglas Home; you could not envisage him as ever having been young. The clothes he wore contributed to this – his middle-aged man's business suit while on duty and his squire-of-the-manor ensemble of checked cap, tweeds and patterned waistcoat when off duty. He never wore what is known now as casual gear, except when he had time off at home watching television and then carried informality to the other extreme, slopping around in

97

an amorphous dressing gown over pyjamas or that most unexciting of garments, a nightshirt.

Interestingly enough it was then, when he was looking his least likely to quicken the heartbeat of a female, that he invariably got the phone calls from women fans sufficiently fascinated by him to go to the trouble of finding out what his ex-directory number was (Brighton 27112). It was an aspect of the loneliness of a famous man that when the phone rang he always used to rush to get to it first, like an out of work actor waiting for the big break. So his secretary did not always have the chance to fend off unwanted calls.

'Women used to phone him and offer themselves to him.' Roger Storey said. 'They would ask him to act out the sexual fantasies they had about him.'

A close friend of Harding told me he once said to him: 'There is no male exclusivity as far as obscene phone calls are concerned. Do you know I have had women phoning me and telling me that they masturbate while looking at me on the screen.' Once when Joan Smith, his housekeeper, got to the phone just after Gilbert had answered it he was holding the receiver away from his ear with distaste. He gave it to her and said: 'Will you handle this woman for me? She's making noises like a recently raped turkey.'

At the studios one female fan was so persistent that commissionaires had forcibly to restrain her outside the entrance when he was broadcasting. It became such a worry that Harding made enquiries about her and when he learned that she worked for a large company he contacted their welfare officer and in that way she was talked into cooling off.

He was sometimes called upon to try to deal with women fans *en masse*. One of his numerous (paid) personal appearances was at the Hammersmith Palais in 1952 when he had been doing *What's My Line?* for barely a year. The occasion was the annual party given by Cope's Pools for more than a thousand young ladies on their staff – the coupon checkers. Sam Heppner had been assigned by the firm handling the publicity to deliver Gilbert to the function sober, but Gilbert never made his speech. When he mounted the bandstand to address the coupon girls assembled on the dance floor they went crazy. 'It was unbelievable, the popularity of that man,' Heppner said. 'The yelling and screaming they did was just as though it was Billy Fury or Marty Wilde or one of the other pop singers of the time. You couldn't imagine anybody more "square" than Gilbert, yet each time he'd try to speak they would break out again.'

Gilbert walked off the platform and into a stiff drink. He had been on his best behaviour, to give Cope's the money's worth of the fee they were paying him, but not through his fault things had wound up as a shambles. At one o'clock in the morning when he got his overcoat to go home he was being baited by two women who formed a well known sister act on the halls in those days. 'They were at their bitchiest,' said Heppner, 'and to try to humiliate him they grabbed his coat and bundled it up and started playing soccer with it in the foyer. I suppose it would be called queer-bashing, although the term wasn't used then. I felt so sorry for Gilbert, standing there watching their performance.'

Gilbert suffered the celebrities' problem of people wanting to touch him. When the celebrity is a sports star, perhaps it makes sense. I recall being with Colin Meads, the formidable New Zealand rugby hero, in the lobby of the Angel Hotel in Cardiff before a big match and a New Zealand supporter came up to him and said, 'Can I feel your muscles?' Permission granted and the man having gone on his way, Meads raised his eyes to the ceiling and said, 'It happens all the time.' But for those not involved in physical conflict . . . 'Why on earth people want to touch me,' Gilbert said, 'is beyond my comprehension.'

Neither could he understand the point in collecting autographs and would either sign reluctantly or make some comment about how aimless it all was. Once when a boy asked him for his autograph he signed three times. When the boy asked why, Gilbert said, 'I understand that at the present market rate, with those three you will be able to get one of Tommy Steele's.'

The late John Pudney, whom we encounter shortly in his role as Gilbert's publisher, told of taking him to a book-signing session at one of the big stores on publication of his life story, *Along My Line*. When he was surrounded 'by hordes of shopping women not likely to buy a copy but bent on touching him or getting autographs', a forceful woman pushed through the crush and held out a cheap Bible she had bought. 'Do you suppose, madam,' Gilbert thundered, 'that I am the author of the Word of God?'

Ray Seaton told me of an encounter with Harding trying to cope with his huge popularity. Seaton, theatre and film critic of the *Wolverhampton Express and Star*, started as a cub reported with the *Leicester Evening Mail* and was sent to interview Harding in that city's De Montfort Hall in the summer of 1953.

'He was of course at the height of his TV fame and known for his irascibility, which was to prompt one or two questions which displeased him.

'When I was ushered into his dressing room before a *What's My Line?* stage show which included Pamela Beeson, Gillian Webb and Johnny Williams, the boxer, with Eamonn Andrews as question master, I found him fuming because a crate – it really was a crate – of whisky had not been delivered to the dressing room. Off he went in search of it, came back after a few minutes looking flushed, and told me that everything had been going wrong.

' "I thought we would never find the damned hall," he said. "It was a ridiculous car journey. How do you find places in Leicester?" I asked him how long it had taken him to find the hall and he snapped: "Long enough to become irritated."

'The previous year he had been quoted as saying that he disliked Leicester's "public face" and when I asked him about this, he affirmed his remark. "But the people who live here don't seem to mind the place," he added.

'I then asked him about his pet hates.

' "None of my hates is pet," he retorted.

' "What *are* your hates?"

' "I haven't any." Then he exploded: "Why am I always being asked asinine questions by reporters? It's silly and unnecessary. People always bother me at the wrong time. Why don't you go away?"

'His mood was very belligerent and I suggested, presumptuously, that if he felt that way he could throw me out and that would give me a much better story. He muttered, walked out of the dressing room and returned two minutes later with a red carnation which he handed to me! His mood was mellowing, but then he became testy because he could not find a pencil. "Oh, all this confusion!" he grumbled.

'On stage, his opening words were: "I hope you welcome me to Leicester. Those who live here are welcome to it."

'Afterwards hundreds of autograph-hunters were at the stage door. Harding turned back when he saw them and walking back up the stairway from the exit, he shouted: "Can't someone get rid of all this nonsense?" It was 9 p.m. "The whole thing should have been over at a quarter past eight," he muttered. "Where's my driver? I'm sick of waiting for people."

'The crowd could not be dispersed. He had to push his way through, refusing to sign autographs. I felt later, on reflection, that he was secretly embarrassed by appearing in public as an entertainer, that he was really demeaning himself; hence his foul mood. But there was charm, too, sudden, unexpected kindliness, as when he gave me the carnation. A peace offering? I don't know. He had certainly been drinking. His colour was high and his speech slightly blurred. His manner was most erratic. But the whole charade was clearly beneath his dignity and he could not bear the sycophancy of the autograph-hunters.'

When I was discussing with Dicky Leeman the disturbed state Gilbert's tremendous popularity got him into, he made a valid point about TV fame and why it created extra problems. Taking an actor as an example, when he was encountered in public there was still that hypothetical barrier of the footlights between him and his admirers. A fan did not go up to Ralph Richardson, for instance, and say 'Hullo, Ralphie old boy, how goes it?' But a TV star was right there in your living room week after week, he was in your home, like one of the family.

The remoteness that existed between members of a large audience in a theatre or a cinema and the performer on the stage or the movie screen had given way to a new era of intimacy between the person on the box and the little cluster of people around it. They were your friends, those stars of television, so when you encountered them in the flesh it was naturally on a first-name, chummy basis – as with David Nixon at the Acropolis.

Gilbert Harding being the first of this new breed – the TV personality – he bore the brunt of this changed attitude. He had no yardstick to go by in coping with the assumption by the public that a television star is just like anyone else who had often been in your home, to be greeted in a pally way anywhere any time. By now the TV personalities who have followed him have learned how to deal with the situation.

For example Penelope Keith, newly experiencing the instant fame of television at the moment, says that she used to enjoy washing her car outside her place. Now she is denied that enjoyment and is put to the expense of having it done in a garage – because a crowd would collect around her. But she just shrugs it off.

Gilbert was never able to shrug anything off, as was the case with a comment from his mother, that expert at the cutting remark. It did not help him to hear the mother to whom he was devoted and to whom he wanted to show up well say to somebody: 'Television seems a silly thing to make him famous.'

CHAPTER 12

SEX AND THE SINGLE MAN

A woman at a party went up to Harding and said: 'Tell me, Gilbert, are you or aren't you queer?' 'No, my dear,' he replied. 'I am merely maladjusted.'

He once wrote: 'My sister didn't marry and I didn't marry and my mother was a widow at thirty, and so when we came to live together we put up a sort of cloud of sexual frustration that was enough to blot out the sun.'

John Freeman, writing of him after his death, said: 'His mother was the only real love of his life.' However, there were at least two other women with whom he spent a good deal of his time. With one of them there was even talk of marriage.

Nancy Spain enjoyed a high reputation among woman journalists of the 1950's. In the same age group as Harding and butch in appearance, she was what might be called a pop-intellectual in view of her rôle as book critic of the *Daily Express* and her incisive writing for other journals, including the magazine *She*, where she was in at the launching with editor Joan Werner Laurie.

She first met Gilbert at a dinner party given by Dilys Powell, film critic of the *Sunday Times*, and her husband Leonard. Recalling the occasion, Nancy wrote that she had been captivated by Harding the conversationalist and by the fact that the stories he told fitted in with her sense of humour. It was the starting point of the Spain-Harding association. The gossip soon got around that they were seeing much of each other and the columnists were quick to hint at romance in the air. However, in view of the fact that Nancy Spain was known for her fondness for those of her own sex and many people being aware of Harding's inclinations, a wit of the time was prompted to remark: 'A love affair between Nancy Spain and Gilbert Harding? That's getting into the realms of science fiction.'

What could have been more romantic for them was a much-publicised shared trip on a banana boat to the West Indies – a slow boat to Jamaica.

Harding's reason for making the voyage was to set to work on his

102

autobiography, commissioned by John Pudney in his capacity as a key man at Putnams. Gilbert was equipped with six stout exercise books, every page of which was to be as unsullied when he returned as when he left. He eventually had four books published, not a single line of which was by his own hand. Of his attempts to write, he said: 'Something goes wrong between my brain and my pen; the words I say in my head are pungent and rounded; by the time they have flowed through my hand they are flat, dull and pompous.' John Pudney has said: 'So remote was he from what appeared under his name that often he would not even read the results of his ghost writers' efforts until the galley proof stage had been reached.'

Even if Harding had seriously intended to put pen to paper on the banana boat to Jamaica he could not have used as an excuse for not doing so the distraction of Nancy Spain being aboard. Not for them the leaning together on the ship's rail watching the ribbon of the moon's reflection scudding along the surface of the sea and the other – in Noel Coward's phrase – 'big romantic stuff' of shipboard life. From start to finish of the voyage their vessel tossed around on turbulent seas threshed at times by gales as furious as Force 10. Harding, perhaps surprisingly, took all in his stride, enjoyed three good meals a day and at all times was in high spirits. Nancy Spain was confined to her bunk, suffering that most depressing, most morale deflating of minor ailments – sea-sickness.

Nevertheless upon their return there was much talk, by the gossips, of marriage and Nancy Spain confessed that the two of them had in fact discussed the subject, over lunch in Antoine's in Charlotte Street. But it had not been with much seriousness. Harding's attitude was: 'It would be a very good idea, but I should want *all* the serial rights.' Finally Nancy Spain answered the match-makers: 'In the heyday of our relationship we could scarcely bear to be parted. We saw each other three and four times a week and fell upon each other's necks when we met. But as the years went by and the mutual attraction ripened (and even decayed a little) we drifted apart. Gilbert went to Brighton; and that was that. I did take a house there, using the excuse that I was going to write a novel, and there were a few crazy evenings in the old style. Champagne until 11 p.m. brandy thereafter, and endless telling of tales. But it would be silly to pretend that Gilbert and I were ever in love with each other in the conventional way.'

Harding's association with Frances Day was somewhat different since that durable blonde – renowned as 'a star of stage, screen and double bed' – was out of a quite different drawer from Nancy Spain.

As totally feminine as Nancy Spain was not, Frannie Day was a veteran sex symbol by the arrival of the 1950s and newcomers in the field like Marilyn Monroe and Brigitte Bardot. A vivacious showbiz personality, she had entertained the troops with wartime revues such as *Black and Blue* and brought glamour to the Crazy Gang. Her off-stage activities being as energetic as her public performances, she had given rise to a well remembered quip by Bud Flanagan. When she had arrived late for a rehearsal looking the worse for wear he had been prompted to comment: 'Little Day you've had a busy man.'

To the objective observer it seemed odd that Gilbert Harding and the ash-blonde bombshell would ever get together. But producers of the type of quiz shows on which he appeared had learned that 'dumb blonde' was something that could not be levelled against her. She was tried and found to be no mean panellist, and Harding and she were often to find themselves sharing a microphone in London and elsewhere around the country.

The out-of-town trip by radio and TV performers to do shows in the hinterland is a well known breeding ground for the budding romance or just plain romp. On the basis that travel heightens sex, the lengthy train ride and the night stopover in a provincial hotel cannot help but bring out the lust in people. So when Harding and La Day were seen to seek each other's company on such jaunts, knowing heads nodded.

They were an ill-assorted couple – the staid looking Gilbert and the breast-waving, leggy Day – but it was felt that obviously they had 'something going'. The truth of the matter was that Harding, for ever seeking stimulating conversation and not often finding it in the showbiz world, enjoyed talking to her. He was to write in one of his books of being 'surprised at her intellect . . . her background of reading and her knowledge of the English poets.'

There was no question of their relationship being on anything but a mental plane, even if Frances Day might have wanted it otherwise. This was borne out on one occasion when the two were at a party and it was decided that some of them would move on to another party. Harding and she shared a taxi and when he was late in arriving at the new venue and was asked what had held him up, he said: 'That Frannie Day – fooling around with my little bit of putty.'

Such transitory dalliance to one side, the lasting devotion of Gilbert Harding's life was undoubtedly his mother.

Psychiatrists would tell you that Gilbert Harding's background was the classic syndrome for production of a homosexual – deprived of his father in infancy and brought up and dominated by his mother. But one must be wary of the pronouncements of psychiatrists. They put all sorts of questions to alcoholics, neurotics, murderers, homosexuals and so on about their upbringing and environment, and come up with explanations as to such people's complexes and behaviour patterns. But they do not spend the same length of time putting the same questions to perfectly normal people. If they did, it would be found that many of the people questioned would give precisely the same sort of answers.

An executive in the steel business whom I know had the same sort of youthful background as Harding. His father died when he was five. He was brought up by his mother, who was even more of a dominating figure than Harding's mother. 'Any girl I brought home,' he told me, 'my mother disapproved of. I had some wonderful girl friends – but each one my mother rejected, telling me "She's not for you." '

This is familiar territory for what psychiatrists tell you produces homosexuals. Did not 'Big Bill' Tilden's mother disapprove of any girl the young tennis star had anything to do with, her over-possessiveness going to the lengths of her saying to him: 'Don't have anything to do with girls. All that will happen is that they will give you V.D.' Tilden molested fellow-Americans on the boat train coming up from Southampton to London for Wimbledon. In the States he became a jailed homosexual following more than one incident, including police in a patrol car flagging down a car weaving along the highway, to discover that Tilden had been masturbating the youth at the wheel.

What happened to the steel man? 'I got out. I couldn't stand my mother's domination any more. I went off and married the girl I wanted to. We have two children, as you know, and we are very happy. My mother wasn't. She hated my wife and made every effort to dominate me until the day she died.'

He was of course but one of countless men who have done the simple thing of withdrawing from the scene. 'My mother made me a homosexual' is merely the 'out' of the homosexual who would have been that way in any event. As a wise general practitioner – not a psychiatrist – once said to me: 'It is not what happens to you in life which makes you what you are. It is how you take it.'

Another doctor said: 'All it really amounts to is that mother domination such as Gilbert Harding experienced *can* result in your being a homosexual but by no means is it necessarily so. And looking at it around the other way, all homosexuals are not necessarily the outcome of being mother dominated.'

It would seem that in regard to the influences which determine that a person will become a homosexual there is some co-operation required from the person concerned. He must want to be a homosexual in the first place.

It puzzles the objective observer why it is that when a man has come under the strong influence of a mother from an early age (in Gilbert's case, the feminine atmosphere was augmented by a sister and two maiden aunts), his sexual interest turns to those of his own sex. The psychiatrists' explanation is that from a surfeit of it he must escape from femininity. One psychiatrist told me that a reason why a man with a mother complex will turn to boys is that 'he wants to please his mother . . . she has a nice boy (himself), so he will do the same, get himself a nice boy.' Well . . .

But *boys* were not Gilbert Harding's interest. If one links the word 'boys' with him when talking to anyone who was in his Weymouth Court coterie, one is immediately corrected – 'Young men, not boys.' Several, separately, said that with Gilbert it was on a high plane, 'Grecian', 'like Plato holding court, the teacher with the young men assembled around him.' Roger Storey said: 'As far as active homosexuality was concerned, Gilbert was about as good at being a homosexual as he was at being a Catholic.'

He tells of Gilbert once reading about the spanking fetish and returning to his flat having bought a hairbrush of the type with a handle. In the course of the evening a young man lowered his trousers and Gilbert went to work with the hairbrush on his bare bottom. After a time he paused and said rather plaintively to another member of the company: 'Am I supposed to be getting a sexual thrill out of this?'

In regard to Harding's homosexuality the point must be made that in this permissive age male homosexuals are 'accepted', to the extent of legislation and a more tolerant attitude towards them, but there are still two aspects which have not gained acceptance. The first is what can be called 'the lavatory scene' and the other is molestation.

As regards the lavatory scene there is no question that many find it distasteful to see men lingering there to pick up other men, but it should be pointed out that the male homosexual is at a disadvantage compared to the lesbian. Men's lavatories are unattractive places to start with, even on the level of a smart hotel or a good pub. Betting shops by law have to be uninviting, functional, with no amenities, to discourage punters from hanging around. Men's lavatories are similarly austere, utilitarian, not by law but because it is not in the male nature to want to spend any but the essential time there.

The female powder room, by contrast, has facilities for lingering – comfortable chairs, wall-tables for make-up and a generally amenable, carpeted atmosphere quite the opposite of the porcelain and tiled-floor male setting. For women, there is a rendezvous quality about the lavatory. Even in the home. There is no conversation in a men's lavatory. Men are in too much of a hurry to get back to the bar, to really worthwhile talk – about racing and football and cricket and get a load of the tits on that one over there by the door.

Also, since lesbianism has never been against the law, there has been no necessity for females to look askance at friendliness in the powder room. The whole atmosphere is conducive to lesbian associations being initiated and furthered. Passes are seen to be made in a women's lavatory. A man can spend a lifetime without seeing the same in a men's lavatory. There the homosexual assignations are as furtive and cheerless as men scanning the girlie mags in a newsagent's.

However, the names of many distinguished males are associated with the lavatory scene. P. N. Furbank, in the first volume of his life of E. M. Forster, discloses that the author of *A Passage to India* hung around public lavatories, 'half-heartedly hoping to make a pick-up'. There was nothing half-hearted about the activities of Tom Driberg M.P. in what he preferred to call the 'cottages', as recorded posthumously in his autobiography. Incidents of this type involving numerous well known actors also have been recorded, mainly in court reports rather than in autobiographies.

Did Gilbert Harding get involved in that aspect of homosexuality? There is no evidence at all to that effect. If one were to discuss it with men who had been intimate friends of his one would get the universal reaction that it was not the type of thing he would do. Many homosexuals do it through a desire to degrade themselves. He had too much class. Also he had a puritanical streak. Tom Sloan tells of arranging to meet him in Paris for a broadcast. When he and Gilbert emerged from the station they were accosted by a man proffering dirty postcards. In the 1950s when pornography, soft or hard, was still not in general circulation in England, the average Englishman on a trip to Paris would show some sort of interest in this, to him, novelty. Not Gilbert. He showered thunderous abuse upon the unfortunate peddler, who hurried out of range of the outburst. Coming out of the studio after the broadcast, Gilbert was accosted by another postcard seller and again was blasted off the scene. Once when Gilbert was at the flat of a female entertainer she said 'Would you like to see my family album?' When she brought it out and opened it on her knees beside Gilbert it was seen to be photographs of the penis (in erection) of each of her more memorable bed partners. Gilbert was shocked.

Gilbert was not that tiresome sort of homosexual who bothers male friends and acquaintants. Few men have not been embarrassed by such approaches at some time or other. Hector Bolitho made a pass at me on a couch at a party in Toronto on the basis, apparently, of our both having worked for the same newspaper in New Zealand. Nor does being engaged in the most manly of sports appear to be any guarantee against homosexuality; a friend tells me that a most vivid memory still stays with him of Max Schmeling surprising him with a probing right hand, not in the boxing ring but under a table at the old Café Royal.

But Gilbert Harding was not of that ilk. No man I have talked to who knew him could ever remember a similar experience. And during the many years I knew him the same thing applied. As a matter of fact, in the course of our numerous contacts there was never any sort of aura of homosexuality to be discerned.

The *effeminate* homosexual is a subject of ridicule, even from other homosexuals. An effeminate pair are called by other homosexuals a 'sister act' or 'bread and bread'. Godfrey Winn died of a heart attack while playing tennis and this prompted a famous cartoonist to produce for private circulation a very sick cartoon depicting Godfrey standing on a cloud with a halo over his head and a tennis racket in his hand, with the caption: 'Anyone for tennis?' And, to continue the tennis theme, Frank Deford in his book *Big Bill Tilden* writes of Tilden being admonished by his friends, 'You're starting to walk like a real fruit', and tells of a series of tennis instructional films he made provoking laughter from the audience at the Tilden walk. Gilbert Harding never gave rise to ridicule in respect of effeminate mannerisms on the TV screen or in private, since they never existed as far as he was concerned.

There was no outward sign in Gilbert's appearance or the way he conducted himself that he was homosexual and that was a reason why there was so much conjecture, even among people who knew him quite well, as to whether in fact he was so. The recurring comment on Gilbert was that he was 'a suppressed homosexual ... he's not a practising queer'. He was in fact a practising homosexual.

Among homosexuals the act of sodomy is not, as might be thought, the pervading scene. A homosexual who has written more than one book on the subject told me: 'It is no more common than the equivalent among heterosexuals.' Masturbation in its various forms is as far as the large proportion of homosexuals go. This was the case with Gilbert. The very thought of the act of sodomy revolted him. He described himself as 'an anti-penetrationist'. It became such a hang-up with him that it extended to symbolism.

Bill Thomson tells of being at the Twickenham flat one afternoon when Gilbert, the man who loved to cook, was preparing a chicken dinner. He called Thomson into the kitchen. It was obvious he had reached the stage of stuffing the chicken. He indicated the mixing bowl. 'Do it for me, will you, dear boy?' said Gilbert. 'I can't bring myself to put it in there.'

To Gilbert, having sexual intercourse with a woman was – psychologically – making love to the one he loved most in the world, his mother, and that was unthinkable. He *did* have normal sex on at least one occasion. Bill Thomson remembers a weekend a group of them spent at Le Touquet, that short hop across the Channel for the casino tables and other attractions being a popular thing to do in those days to escape the drab life in Britain. In the party was a young woman whom Gilbert called 'Miss Marmalade' because her surname was the same as a famous brand. Miss Marmalade took a shine to him and they were seen to withdraw to her room at their hotel. Some time elapsed, during which she was apparently a determined and persevering young lady, for when Gilbert emerged it was made clear that coition had been achieved. Gilbert turned to Thomson and with the look of a small boy who has just had his first taste of ice cream the 45-year-old star of radio and television said: 'It's rather nice, isn't it?'

As far as Gilbert was concerned, however, it did not prove habit forming. When he died one of the Sunday papers 'revealed' that 'past illness' had robbed him of his masculinity... 'unreachable' for him was marriage and its delights, the producing of a family... 'he was impotent'... and his only solace was 'the amnesia of alcohol'.

The story was rather sketchy on facts. For one thing, he had been anaesthetising himself regularly with alcohol from an early age. The paper got sterility mixed up with impotence. Certain illnesses can cause sterility. A grown man contracting mumps, for example, can make him unable to have children. But impotence – the inability to get an erection – is psychological and cannot be brought about directly by an illness. It does not render a man incapable of reproducing. (James Thurber, in a letter to a friend: 'Yesterday I had the disturbing experience of ejaculation without erection.')

One of England's foremost stage and screen actors of between the wars was more philosophical about it all. Jack Hirschberg, onetime publicity man for Paramount in Hollywood, told me that one of their stars whom he liked best was the late Sir Cedric Hardwicke. What endeared Sir Cedric to him from the outset was his saying, 'My name is not really Sir Cedric Hardwicke – it's Sir Seldom Hardprick.'

To a man as sensitive and introspective as Harding it weighed heavily upon him, the fact that, as Freud put it, 'the image of Mother as the love partner cannot help but cause sexual malfunction.'

A man in his late thirties who had been in his teens when he knew Gilbert gave me a more down-to-earth explanation: 'Impotent? The truth of the matter was that Gilbert was always so pissed he could never get a hard on.'

As mentioned earlier, Fleet Street reporters had flocked to Brighton immediately after Gilbert Harding's death and had tried, unsuccessfully, to get stories of his picking up young men in the town. They would have been just as unsuccessful if they had done so in the area of his London flat. As in Brighton, he had plenty of young men in London whom he could, and did regularly, entertain at Weymouth Court.

It was when doing a BBC broadcast or personal appearance out of town that he had need of picking up a young man to share his company. There is nothing exclusively homosexual about that pattern of behaviour. Will not any sexually normal broadcaster, commercial traveller or office desk-jockey 'out of town on business' see what is available in bars and clubs to take back to his hotel bedroom and make it look more lived-in? From the safe ground of normality men condemn the homosexual's choice of company in such circumstances. Terrible for an unmarried homosexual to take a youth to his room; it is perfectly all right for the married man to cheat on his wife by taking to his room the hotel barmaid intercepted on her way up to the staff quarters under the rafters.

However, putting such moral judgments to one side, it is probably true to say that the homosexual is far more likely to be courting trouble by a pick-up than is his normal counterpart. For one thing, he is more likely to contract V.D. since it is more prevalent among homosexuals than heterosexuals for the reason that they are far more promiscuous, not having any fears of pregnancy. But there is also another sort of trouble.

Men usually regard homosexuals as 'harmless', because of the strain they have of feministic weakness. But among the male prostitutes and the semi-pros who hang around the pubs and the 'cottages' there are villains to be found who prey upon the homosexuals.

One of Harding's unfortunate experiences came one day when he went up to Edinburgh to do an edition of *Round Britain Quiz*, checked in at the North British Hotel and phoned the studio to let them know he had arrived. Shortly before broadcast time, however, he phoned them again to say that he had a problem as to how to get to the show – he didn't have any clothes.

'How on earth could that be?' he was asked.

'Stolen,' he said.

'But surely you couldn't have the clothes you're wearing stolen off your back.'

'It's rather more complicated than that,' said Harding.

'Complicated in what way?'

'There's no time to go into that now. Just get some clothes to me here at the hotel or otherwise I'll never make it.'

The puzzled producer found someone in the office of much the same build as Harding and got him to take some of his clothes to the hotel. This done, Gilbert duly went on the air.

What had been the complication? After he had booked in at the North British, Harding had gone for a stroll and had picked up a young man in one of the bars in Waverley Station and taken him to his room. The youth turned out to be a villain. While Harding was having his usual pre-broadcast bath he not only 'rolled' Gilbert for all his money and valuables but also stuffed his clothes into the suitcase and made off with the lot – including the *Round Britain Quiz* questions and answers.

Thus are homosexuals at the mercy of the young men they pick up. What could Harding, stripped in all ways, do about it? He could not phone down to the hotel lobby and get them to intercept the youth making off with his belongings. He could not bring the police into it. Either way there would be embarrassing questions as to what the young man was doing there in the first place.

Once he had put on his make-shift attire the only constructive thing he could do was get the producer to phone the BBC in London and tell them the questions and answers had been unavoidably mislaid. They were phoned through to Edinburgh in time for the broadcast and nobody at Broadcasting House ever learned the full story of how they came to be lost.

Another occasion, this time also while he was doing the *Round Britain Quiz* programme, was when he was in Bristol and Eric Dehn, chairman of the local branch of the English-Speaking Union, wanted him to give a talk to the members. It was arranged that he should meet Gilbert after he had finished at the studio, in one of the better pubs in the centre of the city.

Dehn arrived to find him at the bar with a young Jewish boy. Gilbert had already set the local customers somewhat on edge when he had wandered into the powder room and, realising his mistake, said 'Ladies, I hope you are enjoying your sexual seclusion' and withdrew. Now an argument with the young man got rather out of hand, developing into noisy hostility. When the manager, who clearly prided himself on his elegance, came on the scene Harding rashly addressed him as 'Madam' and they were asked to leave. The young man went out and Gilbert followed, but only after he had delivered an oration of some eloquence to the manager and the assembled customers. On his arrival outside, the youth launched a physical attack on him.

Eric Dehn, a man with a natural inclination to avoid fisticuffs, felt that he must make an exception in this case and he intervened on the side of the distinguished visitor to Bristol, with the result that the boy turned on *him*. Obviously it was time to find a policeman but when Dehn went in search of one the boy pursued him, all round what was then the gracious open square of the city centre, with no policeman

111

to be found. However, Dehn did manage to find a taxi and in this he returned to the pub to pick up Gilbert, who was sitting dejectedly on a bench outside, clutching the boy's scarf.

On the way to the Grand Hotel, where he was staying, Gilbert was effusive in his praise of how Dehn had saved his life. He would return to Bristol and give a talk at the English-Speaking Union for him as a token of his esteem. In the lobby of the Grand, which was then *the* hotel in Bristol, he asked for two pints of beer to be sent up to his room. He was told that it was outside licensing hours, a drink could not be served to a non-resident. He looked at the clerk and said firmly: 'Send two pints of beer to my room. I am a resident and I am extremely thirsty.'

When the two men were in his room one pint of beer was brought to him. He emptied it into the washbasin and said: 'I shall leave this inhospitable inn.' He started packing and was indeed to leave the hotel.

'In his room before he left,' Dehn recalls, 'he still had the boy's scarf. He picked it up and looked at it for a moment or two. Then he opened the window and threw it out.'

A matter of a few hours after Gilbert died the *Daily Sketch* presses were rolling with the headline SECRET FEAR OF GILBERT HARDING, and the lead:

> *Gilbert Harding feared women. That was the secret behind his can-tankerous, grouchy personality and it was a fear he described to a group of intimate friends at a party last Christmas as 'bordering on pathological dislike'.*
>
> *'I fear women because they make me feel so gauche and shy. When I was young I dreamed of being a confident, distinguished lover of beautiful women. But I've never entered a room where there were women without shuddering inwardly. I'd sneer and be cynical as a defence against them . . .'*

The *Sunday Pictorial* followed with HARDING—THE SECRET OF HIS LIFE:

> *. . . He tried to avoid contact with women. 'I cannot bear women near me,' he would say . . .*

One must remember that the homosexual taboo was still very rigid. So, how to get across to readers the 'dark secret' of Gilbert Harding's life? The way to do it, of course, was by implication. He avoided contact with women, therefore draw your own conclusions . . .

The effect the presence of women can have on a homosexual was borne out for me when I was interviewing Somerset Maugham for a magazine piece at the only time he could give me – while sitting for the bust Epstein was doing of him. At one point I – along with Epstein and the photographer with me – was enthralled by something Maugham was telling me (it unfolded as smoothly as one of his short stories), when two people came into the studio to make arrangements for a sitting. Epstein introduced them to us and then asked them whether they would mind waiting until he had finished some aspect of the bust he was working on. They were two princesses of arresting beauty, accentuated by the femininity of their exquisite saris. Maugham resumed his story and I suddenly realised that the stammer which one had so often read about had not previously been in evidence at all. Now, however, it markedly interrupted his flow of words.

But it would be nonsense to say that that reaction was the direct outcome of Maugham's homosexuality. One does not have to be homosexual to feel 'gauche and shy' in the presence of women, as heterosexual males by the dozens will confirm.

The assertion that Gilbert had a dislike of women that bordered on the pathological and that he tried to avoid contact with them was not borne out by the facts. As examples to the contrary there was his close association with Nancy Spain and with Frances Day and there were numerous other women whose company he actually sought and with whom he was completely at his ease. Madeleine Scott, for a time wife of his Cambridge companion Christopher Saltmarshe, was a dear friend. She wrote to me from her home in Malaga: '. . . there was of course never anything between us but I have so many memories of him, many of them of his genuine kindness and unexpected gentleness, not a few of them amusing. I remember what he used to do with the Christmas cards which poured in each year. He would write "and Gilbert Harding" after the sender's name and post them off to other people. I remember him staggering blind drunk into 'The George', in South Kensington, and announcing: "I've just come from a meeting of Alcoholics Anonymous" . . . I remember he took no evasive action at all from one particular person who could have been said to have been all woman – Mary B., who was Toronto's most spectacular nymphomaniac during his time in that city. They got on famously, on a sort of jokey basis. I recall one evening at the Yacht Club hearing Mary, clad in an evening gown with a low-and-behold neckline, announce that she was going out for a stroll in the club's lakeside gardens and a cluster of men also deciding what a good idea it was to get some fresh air. Gilbert watched them as they went off and said, 'Off she goes in a cloud of lust.'

The simple fact of the matter was that he was interested in the sexuality of women (he said of a girl who had a meteoric rise to fame in broadcasting, 'The story of her success is an open bed') but he had no personal interest in them sexually. In this respect he related an incident that had occurred when he was at Cambridge, involving an American undergraduate friend of his named Sonnie Burns, who was excessively fat and had many girl friends. Far from repelling them, his bulk seemed to attract every type from barmaids and waitresses to the students of Girton and Newnham. One day when Gilbert was with Sonnie Burns on Clare Bridge a punt came drifting towards them in which were two girls, one of whom was a peer's daughter, which to an American made her especially intriguing. With a cry of 'Yoo-hoo!', Sonnie jumped from the bridge and landed in the punt, putting his foot through a floorboard, at which it promptly sank. Observing them from the bridge floundering in the water, Gilbert expressed himself as 'thankful for once that I was not smitten by feminine charms.'

However, Roger Storey said that he confided in him that he would have loved to have had a wife and children. One evening they were watching a TV programme which featured Jacqueline Mackenzie, a name which will be remembered by those who were television viewers in the 1950s, and Gilbert said that he felt she would make the ideal mother.

He *could* have married. Charles Laughton did and his wife, Elsa Lancaster, learned of his homosexuality in a shattering way. He had come home one evening and when the front door bell went it was a boy demanding the money Laughton had promised him for services rendered. Elsa Lancaster was confronted with the decision as to whether to be revolted by the whole thing and leave him, or to be understanding and stay with the man she had married because she loved him and admired his great talent. She chose the latter and they were together until he died, without it ever coming to public notice at that time that her husband was a homosexual.

This was revealed with her full consent in a recently published life of Laughton and in the permissive society of today there have been a succession of well known men whose homosexuality has been made public either voluntarily by themselves or by their biographers. These include books by or about Emlyn Williams, Noel Coward, Somerset Maugham, Bill Tilden, E. M. Forster, Lorenz Hart, Christopher Isherwood, W.H. Auden, Tom Driberg.

A reviewer of Tom Driberg's autobiography, published posthumously, made a valid point. Driberg had intended the book to come out in his lifetime, as Isherwood's has. It goes into similarly unrelenting detail about homosexual encounters with grubby young men on a social plane far beneath theirs. Heterosexuals have escapades with sleazy females they prefer to forget about afterwards; why, the reviewer

114

wondered, do homosexuals think that the parading of their sordid couplings makes interesting reading matter?

The heterosexual male indeed keeps occasional visits to the seamy side of sex very much to himself, as a rule not relating any such incident to anybody unless it has the merit of humour. A stockbroker of my acquaintance told me of his lingering rather too long at a pub to which he had gone for an after-work drink and finding himself involved with the barmaid prior to his returning to his wife and loved ones in the Surrey stockbroker belt. When they got down to cases in his car he was sufficiently eager for action as to at once delve deeply south of the border, whereupon she exclaimed: 'Tits first, I'm not common!'

The revelations of a man such as Emlyn Williams in his lifetime had no counterpart in the days when Gilbert Harding was in the public eye. *His* autobiography, naturally enough for the 1950s, contained no hint whatsoever of this important aspect of his life. In 1961 when the book about him by his friends was published the homosexual taboo was still strictly in force. The foreword claimed it would 'constitute a portrait of Gilbert Harding, warts and all'. It did not. So strict was the avoidance of giving the reader any inkling of the then un-mentionable that Michael Noakes told me he had to delete from his contribution a passage referring to Gilbert often conferring with male friends while in the bath, because it might imply you-know-what.

In that pre-permissive era the only way it was ever revealed that a celebrity was homosexual was as a result of a court case. *The Times* of October 22, 1953, reported that 'John Gielgud, aged 49, described on the charge sheet as a clerk . . . was fined £10 at West London yesterday on a charge of persistently importuning male persons for an immoral purpose at Dudmaston Mews, Chelsea. He pleaded guilty.'

After his trial, Gielgud decided he would go on as usual in the play in which he was appearing, *A Day By the Sea*. Dame Edith Evans was in the cast and before he arrived at the theatre she called the others together and said that clearly it was very embarrasing for him and the best thing to do was to behave as though nothing had happened, say not a word to him about it. This was agreed and in due course Gielgud arrived backstage. Edith Evans went up to him and, wagging a finger at him, said with a cheery smile: 'Who's been a naughty boy?'

Gielgud's first entrance in the play was greeted with a round of applause from the audience, undoubtedly not to indicate that they felt he had done something laudatory but to let him know that as far as they were concerned they would not hold it against him.

We know how disturbed Gilbert was about his homosexuality. Would the soul searching and feelings of guilt which plagued him have been alleviated if he had been living in this new permissiveness?

It is right out in the open now, especially in *his* medium – television – which has become the shop window for those now termed gay. We have seen on the small screen *The Naked Civil Servant* with explicit scenes of homosexuals in bed together . . . the camera crews have gone into the gay clubs to hear the views of the ardent readers of *Gay News*, no longer depicted in anonymous silhouette . . . in a TV interview a leading member of the *Monty Python* team gratuitously offered the information that he was homosexual, that he is all for homosexuality and more people should take it up . . . a prestigious David Mercer television play had an all-gay cast . . .

This is all in striking contrast to the swept-under-the-carpet atmosphere of Gilbert Harding's time, but if he were alive now it is doubtful whether it would have made any difference to him.

Gilbert Harding was so sensitive, so easily hurt, emotional and introspective that while the gays prance in the limelight, if he were alive today he would still be tortured by his guilt feelings. As John Freeman said of him, 'he was just about the most deeply miserable man I have ever encountered', and the advent of the permissive age would not have changed that.'

CHAPTER 13

'I AM NOT AFRAID OF DYING'

Those who went into raptures in the 1960s about David Frost as a television interviewer failed to give credit to a man who had brought the in-depth interview to a fine art long before he came on the scene. John Freeman had cut his teeth on the original *Panorama* programme in the early 1950s, and in 1957 he was given his own series – *Face to Face*. He was to become editor of the *New Statesman* and later Ambassador in India and then in Washington, finally to become top man of one of the commercial TV channels, but it was as a television interviewer that he made his impact on the general public.

The Freeman technique on *Face to Face* was absolutely unemotional and as such the antithesis of Frost's dramatised hounding of his subjects and Robin Day's aggression. As Fielden Hughes put it, 'The words came from John Freeman like dripping icicles.' Nevertheless, prominent people of the time hastened to lend themselves to the programme – Lord Morrison, Adlai Stevenson, Tony Hancock, Dame Edith Sitwell, King Hussein, Stirling Moss, Lord Reith – despite the fact that the fee was a miserly fifty guineas. It was a flat fee, nobody was ever paid any more, which was what Evelyn Waugh was told when he was approached. Waugh let it be known, through his agent, that that was not worth considering as far as he was concerned.

'How much did you have in mind?' asked the BBC contract man, doubtless thinking in the back of his mind that he would be asked for 100 guineas.

'Five hundred guineas,' was the simple answer.

The BBC paid up, but not without imposing the strictest security on the transaction to ensure that none of the others ever learned of it.

One programme, however, stood out from the Waugh interview and all the rest and is still vividly remembered by all those who saw it. It was a television 'happening' that became the talk of the nation. Freeman's interview with Gilbert Harding presented the unusual spectacle of a famous person shedding his public image and being reduced to tears.

Robin Day in his book *Television* wrote: 'Can there be any truth in the notion that the television camera exposes public figures for what they really are? All television can do is examine "public" personality. It can rarely strip off the public mask. Occasionally a TV appearance may bring out some flash of a man's inner self, as in John Freeman's *Face to Face* interview with Gilbert Harding. This was a rare case and a unique subject.'

What happened was that in the course of the questioning there was this exchange:

Freeman: *Have you ever been afraid of dying?*

Harding: *I'm not afraid of dying. I should be very glad to be dead, but I don't look forward to the actual process of dying.*

Freeman: *Have you ever been with someone who was dying?*

(Harding breaks down.)

It was made clear in the wide press coverage next day that 'Harding's emotion was taken to refer to his mother's death.'

I learned from Brian Masters that what was not revealed was something that could not have become general knowledge at that time because only Harding and a few intimate friends he had confided in knew about it. It was what had transpired when he saw his mother dying.

He had gone to the nursing home that afternoon to visit her and his way had been blocked outside her room. The medical people under whose care she was told him she was at the end of her life, it would be better for him not to see her in that condition, better to remember her as he had known her. And besides, she was in coma, she would not be able to recognise him or talk to him. He insisted that he see her. They tried to restrain him in his own interests. Forcibly he pushed them aside and went in.

As he stood at the bedside, miraculously she regained consciousness.

'Don't die,' he pleaded with her. 'You can't die and leave me all alone.'

'That's right, Gilbert,' she said, 'think only of yourself. You'll go to the end of your days thinking only of yourself.'

It was this that he remembered when John Freeman asked him the leading question and this that reduced him to tears in front of the television cameras.

The interview had been in September 1960. Two months later Harding died.

On the evening of November 16 1960 Harding had completed two new editions of *Round Britain Quiz*, oddly enough the show which had first brought him to public attention a little over ten years previously. The recordings were done in one of the BBC's overflow studios, at 5

Portland Place, directly opposite Broadcasting House. As he was coming out of the building he collapsed on the entrance steps.

The Times was the only one of the national papers in which Harding's death did not make banner headlines on the front page ... and that was merely because *The Times* was still then adhering to its old world look with advertisements on the front page. Inside, however, they gave the story prominence, climaxing their opening paragraph with: 'Only his chauffeur was with him when he died.' It was a touch worthy of the popular press. His epitaph in one simple sentence: the man who made so many enemies with his rudeness died without a friend at hand. But in point of fact it was inaccurate. He had collapsed into the arms of a friend of his Cambridge days, Christopher Saltmarshe, a BBC current affairs producer.

Harding had walked to the studio after having lunch in his flat in Weymouth Street and the recordings were made with him in the chair and Professor Thomas Bodkin and H.E. Howard representing the Midlands against Cedric Cliffe and Hubert Phillips, for London. From time to time during the session Harding complained of feeling 'absolutely awful'. He was perspiring profusely. 'I'm hot,' he said. 'I don't know why these studios have to be so beastly hot.'

On his desk was his oxygen mask and a bottle of whisky, both of which he resorted to frequently. But the others in the studio were aware of his professionalism. When the recording red light was on he smoothly conducted the programme, made appropriate jokes and gave no indication to the listeners who would be hearing the show that he was in anything but top form.

Immediately the recordings were finished Harding went to the control room and phoned his driver, David Watkins, to bring the car around. Christopher Saltmarshe, in his office on the floor above, hearing that Gilbert was in the building, came down to join the group as they had the usual post-broadcast chat, which soon veered around to what was most topical at that moment: the *Lady Chatterley's Lover* case, in which the publishers of an unexpurgated edition were to be cleared of an obscenity charge. When Harding was told his car had arrived he invited Saltmarshe to come around to his flat for a drink and the two of them left the studio.

Saltmarshe said afterwards that there was no warning of what happened next. They had reached the front steps when Harding just collapsed, falling back into his arms. The driver, standing at the parked car, automatically grabbed the oxygen machine always kept handy in the car and rushed with it to the steps. A knot of office workers going home looked on as he started to bring it into use but it was too late. He and Saltmarshe carried the bulky figure back into the building.

A doctor was called and then Harding's own doctor came on to the scene. He shook his head sadly and said, 'It was inevitable.'

Harding being known to have been a devout Catholic, a priest had been called but when at length he arrived he said that he could not administer the last rites, since it was no avail if not done within half an hour of death. No one was irreverent enough to ask who had set the time limit.

A woman who had been a BBC secretary at the time told me: 'That evening will always stay in my mind. I was working in the building but knew nothing of what had happened on the front steps. I went to the cafeteria for some coffee and was annoyed when I found it shut. I argued with the woman at the door, saying it was always open at that time. She said it was shut and that was all there was to it. I was so persistent that eventually, without saying anything, she opened the door and I was able to look in. Two tables had been pushed together and Gilbert Harding's body was laid out on them while they were waiting for the ambulance. I shall never forget that sight.'

In the previous year, in his capacity of columnist for the *People*, Harding had launched the Gilbert Harding Christmas Fund. At his death so near to a new Christmas, it was decided to change it to The Gilbert Harding Memorial Fund. Contributions topped the £30,000 mark.

Less than three years later a model of Harding in the Brighton Wax Museum was boiled down to make one of Christine Keeler.

INDEX

121